# Mississippi Headwaters GuideBook

"Rivers have what man most respects and longs for in his own life and thought—
a capacity for renewal and replenishment, continual energy, creativity, cleansing."
—*John M. Kauffmann, EPA Journal. May 1981*

The mighty Mississippi River begins its long
journey through these rocks at Itasca State

# MISSISSIPPI HEADWATERS GUIDEBOOK

*Text by* Molly MacGregor
*Photography by* Doug Ohman & Dominique Braud
*Creative/Managing Director* Chip Borkenhagen
*River Maps & Fish Illustrations courtesy of* Minnesota Department of Natural Resources

## MISSISSIPPI HEADWATERS GUIDEBOOK

For information, write to:
Mississippi Headwaters Board
Cass County Government Building
P.O. Box 5
Backus, MN 56435.
cass.mhb@co.cass.mn.us
www.MississippiHeadwaters.org

Published and Edited by Mississippi Headwaters Board & RiverPlace Communication Arts
Mississippi maps, courtesy of Minnesota Department of Natural Resources
Published in association with Minnesota Department of Natural Resources
Funded in part by Central Minnesota Initiative Foundation

ISBN: 978-0-9831785-1-4

RIVERPLACE
COMMUNICATION ARTS
201 West Laurel Street
Brainerd, MN 56401
www.Riverplace-MN.com

The Mississippi Headwaters Board was established in 1980 under Minnesota Statutes 103F.361-378 *to identify and protect the natural, cultural, scenic, scientific and recreational values of the Mississippi River's first 400 miles.* Visit www.MississippiHeadwaters.org for more information. All referenced web addresses/links are "hot-linked" on our website.

Information in this book is presented by using the Minnesota Department of Natural Resources mapping system of the river. Each of these section maps are available at no charge as PDF formatted maps available at www.dnr.state.mn.us/watertrails/mississippiriver/index.html. Printed maps are available at info.dnr@state.mn.us Be sure to check out our Resources Listing on page 79 for further helpful information.

The 5 DNR sections (and maps included in this book) of the Headwaters region are identified by the white boxes on the map below.

## TABLE OF CONTENTS

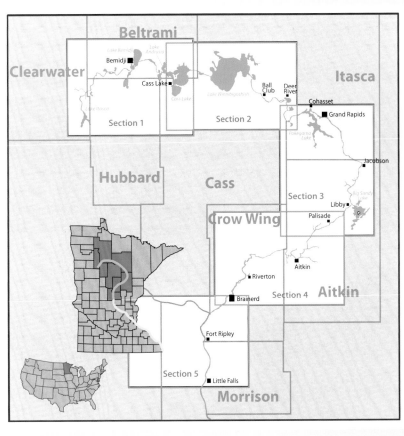

"In a country where nature has been so lavish and where we have been so spendthrift of indigenous beauty, to set aside a few rivers in their natural state should be considered an obligation."
—*Senator Frank Church*

The Mississippi heading north from Lake

# INTRODUCTION

A single raindrop is hardly noticeable. Many raindrops gather into rivulets that cut through soils as they flow across the land, finding paths and also shaping those paths. When the rains end, a river remains: a mix of the rainwater and the material it has moved from the landscape. The channel and the water it holds is a source of life and a refuge for living things. It is a community of many places, all linked together by this meandering artery of water.

This is a guide to the first four hundred miles of the Mississippi River. These miles are the river's headwaters, from its beginning at Lake Itasca, downstream to the city of Little Falls. This guide will take the reader through the river's natural setting as well as the communities that populate the river. The river defines and is defined by its ecological setting, which, in turn, defines the well-being of the river's communities. This guide is a testament to the significance of the Mississippi River and how it has shaped the environment and our lives in northern Minnesota. The book explores three themes to explain the Mississippi's significance:

**Rivers connect us, through time and landscapes.** The landscape and setting of the Mississippi River were sculpted by glaciers tens of thousands of years ago. The visitor can easily visit sites where the evidence of glaciation is clear. Understanding these geological processes helps us understand how natural processes affect the landscape and how human uses contribute to those changes. Three distinct vegetative communities have evolved since then and the Mississippi Headwaters flow past each—prairies to the west, pine forests to the north, and hardwoods to the south. Finally, we know that people have lived on and near the river at least since the glaciers left. The river connects us with them: the river is something our culture shares with those who came before us, and it is something we share with those

who come after us.

**River management begins in the community.** The Mississippi is a mighty river, large enough that it is known as North America's fourth coast. It changes and is changed by every place it flows through. Keeping the river healthy is a collective act, with each community contributing in a way that fits its setting, its economy, and its people. Each community uses the river and each community is challenged to be a steward of its river resources.

Western Grebe and chick

**Individual actions matter.** In the spring, when the snow melts and rain falls, the river may flood. The high water carries loads of sediment, parts of which are deposited at places where the river slows, such as bends in the channel. In the summer, when it is dry, the river's level falls. Just as the seasons change rivers, the way people manage the land along rivers can change the river. Fertilizers, herbicides, road salts, and other pollutants can leach into the runoff. Removing trees and shrubs from a parcel of land, draining a wetland or swamp, planting crops or paving the surface, changes how water runs off the land. That runoff eventually flows to a river. Runoff can be slowed, or collected, or buffered to help maintain the balance of water and sediment and reduce the chance that the runoff can cause excessive damage.

This book tells two important stories: what individuals and communities can do to enjoy the river and how they can protect the river. It does so by taking a closer look at five sections of the river, each covering about eighty river miles. Each section explores the themes of landscape, people, management, and individual actions to tell the story of the Mississippi Headwaters and to show

*Gichi-ziibi, meaning "Great River" in Ojibwe, is the fourth longest river in the world.*

Trumpeter Swans                    *DOMINIQUE BRAUD*

how its citizens are preparing for the future. By the end of the book, you will have taken a trip down the first four hundred miles of the Mississippi River. In the course of this journey, you will discover how the Mississippi Headwaters defines the landscape, shapes our culture, and most importantly, how we can be stewards of its gifts.

**The Mississippi Headwaters Board provides local control of the first 400 miles of the river.**

Stewardship of the nation's mightiest river is in the hands of the communities through which it flows. Rivers have a variety of values important to us: the natural setting, the cultural significance, scientific knowledge, scenic beauty, and recreational uses. Managing rivers requires attention to each value and, requires attention from each of us who uses the river. Thus, successful river management starts with the community and the individuals who populate that community. That's why, for thirty years now, the Mississippi Headwaters Board has protected the natural and human values of the Mississippi's first four hundred miles. It might not have been this way. In 1975, the

*DOMINIQUE BRAUD*

Lake Itasca and its park are
Minnesota's crown jewels.

"The song of the river ends not at her banks
but in the hearts of those who have loved her."
—*Buffalo Joe*

Little Falls Pa

federal government determined that the headwaters of the Mississippi River were eligible for inclusion in the National Wild and Scenic River System, a designation reserved for outstanding free-flowing and undisturbed rivers, such as the St. Croix.

Because the National Wild and Scenic Rivers Act protected natural conditions, it literally drew a line around the river and its riparian lands and set those lands aside from further development. That approach was not considered feasible in northern Minnesota. The Mississippi River had been the backbone of the region's commerce—first during the fur trade, later for logging and hydroelectricity, then transportation, and more recently for fishing, recreation, and drinking water. When the federal government proposed setting aside the Mississippi Headwaters, the eight

counties on the river answered back, "Let us manage the river."

The state was applying a similar concept to the six rivers it had designated as wild and scenic. Unlike the federal approach, the Minnesota approach used local land-use law to manage development of river shore land. The Minnesota Legislature delegated to the counties the authority to plan for protection of the Mississippi's natural, cultural, scenic, scientific, and recreational values in the unincorporated areas, and to administer a common zoning ordinance to assure local development met the intent of the plan. The counties administered the land use rules and the new board was empowered to review and certify county actions.

Each member county appointed a commissioner to the new board. Finalized in 1980, the proposal was endorsed by the National Park Service, enacted into Minnesota statute in 1982, and funded by the state, with matching funds from the counties. The eight counties signed on and the Mississippi Headwaters Board was established.

In 1988, the Mississippi Headwaters Board added a volunteer water quality monitoring program to its activities. Measuring water quality would help determine if the river management rules were protecting the river's health. Monitoring the biological, chemical, and

*The Mississippi River travels 2,552 miles to the Gulf of Mexico.*

*It would take a drop of water about three months to travel from Itasca through New Orleans.*

physical aspects of water quality was a way to demonstrate that river management was effective, the Board reasoned.

The program used professional equipment, methods, and standards to measure several parameters of river health. Students in high school biology, chemistry, and even agriculture classes were trained by River Watch staff to use the equipment. All participants also engaged in quality assurance and quality control, not only to understand how professional scientists work, but to assure that the

Educational challenges and opportunities are bountiful within the Mississippi Headwaters Board's spheres of influence.

data collected by student monitors would be used by the state's water quality agencies. Matching water quality to river protection added a new level of information, grounded in science, to local decision-making.

Linking water quality to local management makes sense, since the condition of riparian lands drives water quality. Since the 1970s, cities and industries significantly reduced pollution from point sources, or pollutants discharged from wastewater treatment pipes. Today, water bodies can be pol-

luted by "nonpoint sources," which occurs when stormwater moves sediment and nutrients from the landscape to water bodies. In a natural setting, topography and vegetation soften the force of stormwater. Filling low spots, removing plants, and "hardening" the surface by paving increase the amount of water running off the landscape.

Addressing the problem of nonpoint source pollution happens parcel-by-parcel, landowner-by-landowner. Individuals and communities can apply remedies to nonpoint source pollution and

the community can monitor water quality to measure the effectiveness of their actions. This is the Mississippi Headwaters Board's program of river management: guide the development to manage the effects of stormwater runoff and empower the community to monitor the effectiveness of that management.

*PHOTOS FROM MISSISSIPPI HEADWATERS BOARD FILES*

"When despair for the world grows in me and I wake in the night at the least sound in fear of what my life and my children's lives may be, I go and lie down where the wood drake rests in his beauty on the water, and the great heron feeds.
I come into the peace of wild things who do not tax their lives with forethought of grief. I come into the presence of still water. And I feel above me the day-blind stars waiting with their light. For a time I rest in the grace of the world, and am free."
—Wendell Berry, *The Peace of Wild Things*

Sedge grasses filter water and provide essen
habitat for wildlife.

In short, the Mississippi River's unique landscape and history are linked to the power of individual action. It is the sum of our independent actions that protect the river. Our respect for this river is revealed through our commitment to managing our impacts so that the river is a legacy that empowers our children's future.

Snowy Egret

*DOMINIQUE BRAUD*

*Rivers have a variety of values important to us:*
*the natural setting,*
*the cultural significance,*
*scientific knowledge,*
*scenic beauty,*
*commerce and*
*recreational uses.*

Old railroad bridge at Palisade.

*DOUG OHMAN*

"What had been long sought at last appeared suddenly, on turning out of a thicket, into a small weedy opening. The cheering sight of a transparent body of water burst upon our view. It was Itasca lake – the source of the Mississippi River."

—*Henry Schoolcraft*

Lake Itasca

# LAKE ITASCA TO CASS LAKE

This 80-mile river section is where the traveler can really appreciate how our landscape was shaped. It is also a place to learn how the first peoples lived in Minnesota. It is a place to learn what a watershed is and how the lands draining to the river affect its conditions. River management of this section emphasizes opportunities to explore and research the landscape. It is the starting point for the river and for our voyage.

What is a river's headwaters? Simply put, it is an intermittent or perennial stream without tributaries. Scientists use the term "first order" to describe these streams. When two first order streams meet, the merged waters become a "second order" river and, as tributaries join the main channel, it becomes a third order, then fourth order, and so on, until the river empties into a larger body, as the Mississippi does in the Gulf of Mexico. Every large river is fed by hundreds of thousands of small headwater streams; in fact, small streams make up most of the miles in a river's drainage system. Thus, every aspect of the river's condition and quality begins in headwaters streams.

The Mississippi River is also a source of our nation's history. Before the United States became a nation, Europeans sought the source of the Great River, hoping it would prove to be the route to the Pacific, China, and Japan. And, in the early years of the American nation, the source of the Mississippi River was considered the new country's northwest boundary.

The headwaters of the Mississippi River offer the traveler the opportunity to learn important lessons about geology, climate, biology, culture, and history. These lessons provide a context for understanding our relationship to the river today. Simply put, the lessons are these:

- Our landscape was shaped by glaciers.
- Three distinctive biological or ecological regions—prairie, pine forest, and hardwood forest—are found in Minnesota.

- People have lived here for thousands of years.
- The Mississippi River has always been a fundamental part of how people make a living in north central Minnesota.

We'll start with glaciers, which created the landscape over thousands of years. Glaciers occur when the climate is so cold that snow does not melt in the summer. As the snow accumulates, the bottom layers compress into ice. As the weight of the snow mass increases, it exerts pressure on the ice at its base, causing it to flow away from the pressure of the weight. A glacier acts like a conveyor belt moving debris, or like a plow moving material out in front of its ice, dropping piles of rock, sand, and muck, or carving out pathways or holes.

Evidence of these movements can be seen throughout the Mississippi Headwaters region. The landforms created by deposits of glacial ice

*DOUG OHMAN*

One of Minnesota's most iconic images is that of the birth of the Mississippi as it flows through these stones at Itasca State Park.

## LEGEND

| | | | | | | |
|---|---|---|---|---|---|---|
| Carry-in Access | | Campground | | Parking | | Hospital |
| Water Access | | Watercraft Campsite | | Drinking Water | | River Mile |
| Outfitter | | Shelter | | Dam | | Rapids |
| Dock | | Safe Refuge | | Interpretive Center | | |
| Accessible | | Safe Refuge is shelter with access to a telephone | | Point of Interest | | |
| Public Land | | Picnic Area | | Fish Hatchery | | |
| Private Lands | | Fishing Pier | | W.M.A. | | |
| | | Natl Great River Rd | | MN Great River Rd | | |

Interstate Highway     U.S. Highway     State Highway     County Road

North

0  1  2  3  4 miles
0  1  2  3  4 kilometers

W.M.A. = Wildlife Management Area
S.N.A. = Scientific and Natural Area

### Map labels

Bemidji
Grass Lake
Little Mississippi River
Rice Lake
Bootleg Lake
Township Bridge *River Level Gauge*
1290
Power Line
Silver Maple Campsite
Iron Bridge Campsite
1305
1300
Iron Bridge Landing
1295
Fox Trap Campsite
1315
Pine Point Landing
Bear Den Landing
1310
Beltrami County / Hubbard County
Clearwater County
1320
95
Fern Lake
Lake Marquette
Lake Plantagenet
Hennepin Creek
Stumphges Rapids
*Stumphages Rapids*
1325
Mississippi Headwaters State Forest
Coffee Pot Landing
Power Line
1330
*River Level Gauge*
40
Diamond Lake
Becida
Mud Lake
White Earth State Forest
Upper Rice Lake
Bear Creek
1335
Robinson Lake W.M.A.
Robinson Lake
37
Mallard Lake
Mallard Lake W.M.A.
Vekin's Dam *Portage Left 50 yards*
1340
LaSalle Creek
Big LaSalle Lake
Wanagan Landing
Gill Lake W.M.A.
Iron Springs Bog S.N.A.
Gulsvig Landing
Sucker Lake W.M.A.
1345
Culvert *Portage right 30 Yards*
Low Dam
Pine Ridge
Itasca State Park *Vehicle Permit Required*
Lake Itasca
Bear Paw Campground
Elk Lake
38
48
71
1
200
113
71
Clearwater County / Becker County
Hubbard County

---

## ROUTE DES[CRIPTION]

### GENERAL DESCRIPTION OF ROUTE

At Lake Itasca, 2,348 miles from the Gulf of Mexico, 560 miles from Minneapolis-St. Paul, the Mississippi River begins its course. In its first 90 miles, the river winds through ancient lake beds, and occasionally rushes throuh narrow valleys of spruce. At Bemidji, the river flows through the first of several large lakes. This is the most scenic and the most remote of the Mississippi's Minnesota miles.

The paddler needs some skills and patience in this section. There are rocky riffles, snags, and beaver dams to be maneuvered around. Campsites that are accessed from the river only, require wilderness skills. An old logging dam and a working dam must be portaged. However, two state parks, Itasca and Lake Bemidji, offer the visitor many amenities.

Potable water is not always available at campsites. Paddlers are encouraged to carry water treatment systems or their own water. River reading and compass skills are necessary to navigate through the wetland areas. In most cases, follow the downstream flow. Beware of sweepers/strainers in heavily treed areas outside of the wetlands.

River miles are counted upstream from the Mississippi's confluence with the Ohio River, according to a system developed by the U.S. Army Corps of Engineers.

*Note: (R) and (L) refer to right bank and left bank, respectively, when facing downstream.*

**1347.0  Lake Itasca**
The river's outlet at Lake Itasca is man-made. The low dam of stones was built in the 1930s; the river's true outlet is through the swamp, just downstream from the lake. The Headwater History Center at Itasca State Park explains how the headwaters were discovered.

**1346.7  County Road 38 culvert**
Portage right 30 yards.

**1345.0 (R)  Gulsvig Landing**
The Gulsvig family donated land to create this public access where State Highway 200 crosses the river. The family still vacations on the river.

**1342.0 (R)  Wanagan Landing**
Sucker Brook runs through Iron Springs Bog Scientific and Natural Area, a unique spruce forest that is perched above the water table. The cool brook supports trout, and enters the Mississippi upstream of the landing.

**1339.0 (L)  Vekin's Dam/Portage**
Portage left 50 yards. The wooden dam was built during the first part of the twentieth century to assist movement of logs downstream. At this point, the river leaves the wetland and enters a narrow valley.

*Caution: For the next four miles, you will experience Class I rapids, produced by sandbars and rocks. The rapids end at the Clearwater County Road 2 bridge.*

**1338.0  Clearwater County Road 37 bridge**

**1335.5  Clearwater County Road 2 bridge**
The landscape changes back to wetland[...] dams obstruct the river in this section.

**1333.2  Clearwater County Road 40 bridge**

**1330.9  Powerline crossing**

**1330.7 (L)  Coffee Pot Landing**
A river level gauge is located adjacent to [...] bridge. When the gauge reads 3.5 ft. or [...] water level is high; level is average whe[...] gauge reads between 3.5 and 1.9 ft., and l[...] it is below 1.9 ft. Expect conditions to be [...] downstream of Coffee Pot at 1.9 and be[...] Drinking water is available on the right [...]

**1328.2 (R)  LaSalle Creek**
Watch for the tall bank on the right; it is [...] paddle upstream to the first of the LaSal[...]
*Caution: The Mississippi enters a large [...] and finding the channel can be a challen[...] water conditions. This stretch is nearly f[...] miles long.*

**1324.0  Mile Marker**
*Caution: The river enters a narrow spruc[...] In high water conditions, expect Class I[...] for two river miles*

**1323.8–.2  Stumphges Rapids**
Class I rapids for two 1/2 mile segments [...]

**1321.8 (L)  Hubbard County Road 3 bridge and [...] access**
Downstream of this bridge, the paddler [...] another large wetland, extending five m[...] downstream. *Caution: Finding the chan[...] be difficult in low water.*

**1315.5  Beltrami County Road 5 bridge**
A river level gauge is mounted on the b[...] Water level is considered high if the leve[...] than 7.5 ft.; average if it is between 6 an[...] and low if it is under 6 ft., and not canoea[...] the reading is under 4 ft. (portage to Bea[...] the Rice Lake Forest Road). The river [...] and enters another large wetland. *Caution [...] the channel may be difficult in low wate[...]*

**1312.2 (L)  Bear Den Landing**
Access is from Beltrami County Road 5 [...] Rice Lake Forest Road. Paddlers shoul[...] the DNR website for forest road closure[...] planning a trip.

**1311.1 (L)  Fox Trap**
Watercraft campsite only.

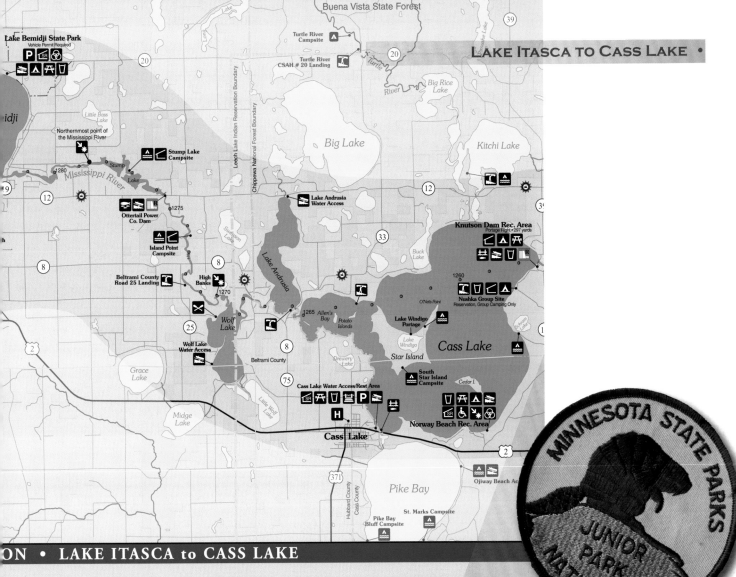

# ON • LAKE ITASCA to CASS LAKE

**(R) Hennepin Creek**
A sand bank opposite the creek's mouth provides an excellent view up and down the Mississippi, and up Hennepin Creek.

**(R) Pine Point**
Road access is on the Stecher Forest Road from Hubbard County Road 3. Paddlers should check the DNR website for forest road closures when planning a trip. *Caution: The river meanders through a large wetland from this point to Iron Bridge Landing downstream. Bog chunks can become dislodged and float downstream. This makes it difficult to find the channel and can be a navigational hazard.* This condition is not dangerous, but it is advisable to call the regional DNR office to determine conditions before planning a trip.

**Rice Lake Channel**
Do not enter.

**(L) Iron Bridge Watercraft Campsite**
This site, accessible by river only, rises above the Mississippi River and provides an overlook to the upstream wetland.

**(R) Iron Bridge Landing**
Water access is from Beltrami County Road 7. The bridge that gave the landing a name was removed in 1984. The river leaves the section designated "Wild" by the Mississippi Headwaters Board, and enters the "Scenic." There's more human development as the paddler approaches Bemidji, 15 miles downstream.

**Township Bridge**
A river level gauge is on the bridge south of Beltrami County Road 7. The river is high when the water level is more than 5.2 ft.; average if the level is between 4.2 and 5.2 ft., and low below 4.2 ft.

**Beltrami County Road 11**
A powerline crosses the river here. The river enters a deeply wooded floodplain forest, where elm and cottonwood arch overhead.

**(L) Silver Maple Campsite**
Located north of Carr Lake, Schoolcraft River flows through Carr Lake from the south; the river parallels the lake's northwest corner and meets its outlet on the lake's north shore. The Schoolcraft River is a state-designated trout stream.

**US Highway 2/Yellowhead Road**
A series of three bridges.

---

**1284.5 (R)  Lake Irving Access**
The paddler now enters the City of Bemidji's business district. *Caution: Submerged pilings by public access. Stay in marked channel.*

**1284.0  City of Bemidji**
If you paddle to the northwest, you will see the city's waterfront and Tourist Information Center building. Stop at the center for information on supplies, food, and lodging. Lake Bemidji derives its name from an Ojibwe word, "Pemidjigumang," maning the river that crosses the lake. *Caution: paddling across the lake is not recommended; if you must do so, stay closer to the shore.*

**Lake Bemidji State Park**
Located on the lake's northeast shore, north of the down river exit of the lake.

**1281.5  Beltrami County Road 19 bridge**
The Mississippi River exits Lake Bemidji at the midpoint of its eastern shore. Extensive bulrush beds mark the river's exit from Lake Bemidji. An old railroad trestle spans the river at the outlet.

**1278.6  Northernmost point of the Mississippi River.**

**1277.1 (L)  Stump Lake Campsite**
The river access campsite is the river's northernmost point. The Ojibwe people called the series of rapids that once constricted the river between Wolf Lake and Lake Bemidji, "Metowsa," or "10."

**1275.7  Otter Tail Power Co. Dam and access**
Portage right. The dam was built in 1909 to provide electrcity to the City of Bemidji, when each household's use was the equivalent of a single lightbulb. Today, the dam's output is less than 1% of the electricity consumed by its customers.

**1275.6  Beltrami County Road 12 bridge**
Expect to see bald eagles and blue herons between here and Beltrami County Road 8 during early summer mornings.

**1273.7 (L)  Island Point Landing**
River access only. Located on a steep, high bank that provides a view upstream of the river to the north. Expect a short section of Class I rapids when water level is average or lower about 0.75 mile downstream.

**1272.9-7  Class I Rapids**

**1272.5  Beltrami County Road 8 bridge**

---

**1271.5 (R)  Beltrami County Road 25 and Water Access**

**1270.0  High Banks**
This location provides a spectacular view of the river and Wolf Lake. Evidence of historic and prehistoric human use exists for this site. Down river exit is located to the left on the northeast corner of Wolf Lake.

**1269.7(R)  Wolf Lake Water Access and Outfitter**

**1267.5  Beltrami County Road 8**

**1266.0 (R)  Lake Andrusia**
A carry-in access is located on the southeast shore. A water access is on the north shore. Mission Point is the land barrier between Andrusia and Allen's Bay of Cass Lake. The site was long used by Ojibwe people and an Episcopal mission was built here in the early 19th. century.

**1264.0  Allen's Bay**
Named by Schoolcraft for Lieutenant James Allen, who accompanied both the 1820 and 1832 journeys on the Mississippi. Allen was an artist and cartographer, his accounts of the trips are published with Schoolcraft's. The Potato Islands are owned by the U.S. Forest Service. *Caution: paddlers are advised to respect the power of the wind on a large lake and stay away from the center of the lake. If you must paddle the lake, stick to the shoreline. The lake can be dangerous, and winds rise unexpectedly.*

**1263.4  Carry-in Access**

**1263.0  Star Island**
Cass Lake's largest island has a lake within it. Star Island is located on the western side of Cass Lake. Parts of the island are public lands.

**City of Cass Lake**
Cass Lake is named for Lewis Cass, who as governor of Michigan, sought the Mississippi's headwaters in 1820. He ended his journey at this lake, then known as Red Cedar Lake, for the trees that dominated its shorelines. Henry Schoolcraft traveled with Cass in 1832. The town of the same name is found on the lake's southwest corner, accessible by the Highway 2 rest area. Stop for supplies, food, and lodging.

---

This marks the down river boundary of this map. Refer to map 2 for the route from Cass Lake to the Vermillion River.

*DOUG OHMAN*

Bemidji enhances its beauty on this bridge display.

are drumlins, kames, and eskers. End or terminal moraines are the debris of boulder, rock, and gravel left at the endpoint of the glacier. Landforms carved out by glaciers are kettles, tunnel valleys, lakes, and wetlands.

The glacial features of the Mississippi's first 80 miles are tunnel valleys and ice block lakes. Tunnel valleys are streams eroded under a glacier by the melted ice water. The Mississippi and the two creeks lying east of the Mississippi—LaSalle and Hennepin—are tunnel valleys. The visitor can observe this formation at Bear's Den Landing or Fox Trap camping spot, just west of the mouth of Hennepin Creek on the Mississippi. A tall sand bank is an excellent observation point.

Climate has changed the region from ice-covered to plant-covered. The climate of the Mississippi Headwaters region has changed dramatically in the thousands of years following the end of the ice era. As the planet's temperature rose a few degrees, the snow melted, lichens and moss drifted into the barren landscape and flourished. The new plants attracted animals that brought new seeds and new growth. The first forest was of spruces and other hardy pines, which had shallow spreading roots that tolerated icy swamp waters. This forest is known as boreal and is actually the largest forest type on the planet, covering the northern regions of North America, China, and Europe.

The perched black spruce bog forest is the

"Boundaries don't protect rivers, people do."
—Aristotle

DOUG OHMAN

type of vegetative community that first flourished in the region after glaciation. The black spruce is a pioneer: one of the first tree species to thrive on wetlands or lakes that are filling in with vegetation. The floor of the forest is dominated by mosses and marked by the wandering, shallow roots of the black spruce tree. The bog is perched: that is, it is separated from the groundwater by an impermeable layer, likely composed of clay. The springs found at the site are rich in iron, as are many of the springs that percolate into the Mississippi River in this region.

Visitors can walk through a black spruce swamp at Iron Springs Bog Scientific and Natural Area. It is located five miles downstream of the headwaters, straddling Sucker Creek, just off Highway 200 west of the Mississippi River. The creek flows north from a lake through an open area vegetated by hummocks of sedge grasses. Black spruce grows a few yards inland from the creek. The roots of the spruce are visible above the forest floor, which is a mat of sphagnum moss. The black spruce creates a closed canopy, blocking sunlight so the interior of the forest is dark, damp, and cool.

Plants have adapted to these unique conditions. The "bog adder's mouth" orchid is the smallest and perhaps rarest of the 43 species of orchids found in Minnesota. It roots in the moss, not the soil, a biological adaptation shared with its tropical forest-canopy-dwelling cousins in the southern hemisphere.

The archaeological record of people living near the Mississippi River begins with the end of glaciation. People may have lived near the river during the thousands of years of the ice age. However, the movement of glacial ice has hidden or scraped away records of any human occupancy.

Archaeologists use the term "Paleoindian" to describe the first people to live near the headwaters as the glaciers retreated 10,000 years ago.

Muskrat

*DOMINIQUE BRAUD*

These people hunted large mammals, such as bison, and likely gathered plants, fish, and small game. Bison hunting was a group activity: the animals were herded towards steep hills and cliffs, often near streams, and killed, then skinned and butchered at the site. Paleoindian bison kill sites are documented south of Lake Itasca, within the Itasca State Park's boundaries, and also at Sucker Creek, just west of the park. The remains of the kills and butcherings include spear and arrow points, flaked knives, choppers, and scrapers.

In the Archaic period, 6000 to 800 years BC, people established settlements at the margins of lakes and streams. Archaic period sites have been documented on LaSalle Creek and on the river between Carr Lake and Lake Bemidji. People hunted large mammals, but they also trapped smaller animals, fished, foraged, processed plants, and made tools and implements. During the Woodland period from 800 BC to historic contact with Europeans, both settlement and plant domestication increased. These people made ceramics and built mounds to bury their dead. Jacob Brower documented mounds, likely built during this era, on the shorelines of the streams and lakes of the Mis-

Bluegill

"To have some parts flowing free...with deer grazing on its banks...ducks and geese raising their young in the backwaters...
eddies and twists and turns for canoeists...and fishing opportunities such as Lewis and Clark enjoyed...
would be the finest possible tribute to the men of the Expedition, and a priceless gift for our children."
*—Stephen Ambrose, Undaunted Courage*

The scenic beauty of this portion of the Misssissippi inspire
meditations on a comforting sense of place we can too ofte
take for granted.

sissippi Headwaters.

Further evidence of human occupation is seen in the river channel itself, which has been altered in several locations. The first is the outlet of the river from Lake Itasca. The rocks that mark the Headwaters are located a few feet northeast of a willow-alder swamp, which is more likely the river's true source. The picturesque rocks of the headwaters were placed by U.S. Works Progress Administration crews in the 1930s. The site must be periodically filled with sand and gravel to prevent the river from returning to its original channel.

The historic record of Europeans at the headwaters begins with Father Hennepin's journey in 1680. In that year, he was one of four French missionaries assigned to the company of Robert Cavalier, Sieur de LaSalle, on his exploration of the Great Lakes. De LaSalle was looking for the Mississippi River and a route across the North American continent to China. Hennepin and three others were separated from the group and traveled with Dakota people to Lake Mille Lacs, where he spent a year—a time that he describes as being held captive. He was ill and injured from his journey up the Illinois River to the Mississippi. However, others in his party traveled with their Dakota hosts north to what Hennepin surmised was the source of the Mississippi River.

The observations of his fellow travelers and his Dakota hosts convinced Hennepin that the source of the Mississippi River was neither the

*John Westly Powell defined watersheds as "that area of land, a bounded hydrologic system, within which all living things are inextricably linked by their common water course and where, as humans settled, simple logic demanded that they become part of a community."*

Gulf of California nor the Pacific Ocean. Nonetheless, Hennepin remained convinced that a traveler could reach the Pacific by following the rivers to the northwest of his location. "But by the help of my discovery, and the assistance of God, I doubt not but a passage may still be found, and that an easy one too," he wrote in one of his three volumes about his journeys. Thomas Jefferson owned each of Hennepin's books about his North American explorations and is said to have drawn on them when he proposed Lewis and Clark's Missouri River journey in 1803.

William Morrison, a fur trader, recorded his visits to Lake Itasca, or Lac La Biche, as the French translated the name, in 1804. Zebulon Pike got as far as Ottertail Point on Leech Lake, arriving there in January 1806. Pike named Leech Lake the Mississippi's source.

Next, Lewis Cass, military hero of the War of 1812 and Governor of the Michigan territory, which included the Mississippi, sought the river's source. The U.S. Department of War financed his expedition. The river's source was considered part of the nation's boundary, so mapping it was a military imperative. Cass traveled west from the Great Lakes via the Savanna Portage and got as far as Cass Lake—Red Cedar Lake then— which he said was the source of the Mississippi River, and thus the northwest boundary of the United States. Henry Schoolcraft was the geologist on this trip.

Giacomo Beltrami visited the headwaters in

*At Lake Itasca, the average water flow rate is 6 cubic feet per second. (44 gallons/second). At Upper St. Anthony's Falls, the northern most Lock and Dam, the average flow rate is 12,000 cubic ft/second (89,869 gallons/second). At New Orleans, the average flow rate is 600,000 cubic feet per second (4,494,000 gallons/second).*

Black Crappie

1823. He was an Italian count who traveled with Major Stephen Long of the U.S. Army's Engineers, and Lawrence Taliaferro, the U.S. Indian Agent at Fort Snelling. The partnership did not last, and Beltrami left the others at the confluence of the Pembina and Red Rivers. He traveled east to the continental divide in what is now Beltrami County, declaring a lake there the ultimate source of the Mississippi and naming it for a much loved deceased friend, Giulia Spada de Medici.

Beltrami was often chided, especially for the red silk umbrella he kept with him on his travels. But he is also remembered as a man of courage. He was without financial prospects in his home country. He had been both a soldier and an official in the Napoleonic government, but left Italy after that government fell and the papal government was restored. He believed in individual freedom, education, and science. His identification of Lake Julia—which still carries the name he bestowed— as the northern reaches of the Mississippi's watershed is geographically accurate. He engaged with both Dakota and Ojibwe people on his travels and brought artifacts home to share. A Native American flute carved from a single piece of red cedar

with the bell end shaped like a fish head now rests in the Museo Civico di Scienze Naturali (Civic Museum of Natural Science) in Bergamo, in Northern Italy.

Beltrami did not represent a government and served no official purpose in his quest, other than his own curiosity. "One comes to America," he wrote, "to see a new world. A river of vast extent, of a majesty which it is difficult to conceive; a country presenting extraordinary features at every step; a race of men entirely different from those of Europe; afford abundance of new and important subjects for philosophical meditation." We may think of Beltrami as an amusing footnote in the history of the Mississippi River, but he was a brave adventurer inspired by the desire to learn and see a new world.

Posterity acknowledges that Henry Schoolcraft fixed the headwaters of the Mississippi River at Lake Itasca as a result of his 1832 expedition. His companions were drawn from a group of soldiers, missionaries, and Native Americans who, like Schoolcraft, made the journey several times. Schoolcraft acknowledged their contribution by publishing their diaries with his.

The first city on the Mississippi celebrates the river as a community—from its University campus on the lake, through the arts, and through its vibrant Chamber of Commerce.

*DOUG OHMAN*

For example, Schoolcraft asked Reverend William Boutwell, one of his traveling companions, to provide the name for the lake. Starting with the Latin words—veritas caput or "true head"—Boutwell dropped the first and last syllables to create "itas ca." By creating a name for the lake, Schoolcraft claimed discovery of the river's headwaters. Each recorded journey to the Mississippi's source was in the company of native people—Dakota and Ojibwe—who knew the area well. The discovery of the Mississippi's true source now answered the question about it being the Northwest Passage to the Pacific Ocean—to the negative—and provided a boundary for the American nation at that time. It also led the way to American settlement of the region, ironically displacing the very people who brought the Americans to the source in the first place.

### Community Management Number 1: Itasca State Park

In 1889, the Minnesota Historical Society commissioned Jacob Vradenburg Brower to survey the sources of the Mississippi River and to determine the true source of the Mississippi River. Brower was a lawyer by training, and a geographer, surveyor, and archaeologist by avocation.

On his 1889 survey, Brower delineated the height of land that defined drainage to Lake Itasca. He joined the voices advocating establishment of a state park at the Mississippi's headwaters. The timing was right. National parks had recently been dedicated at Yosemite in California and Yellowstone in Montana, and a forest preserve created at New York's Adirondack Mountains to protect the Hudson River, the source of New York City's drinking water. Brower cited all of these and noted that the Mississippi River was source for drinking water at Minneapolis and St. Paul. At the same time, Minnesota was entering the most productive decades of its lumbering years and Brower wanted

*DOUG OHMAN*

to protect the forests at Lake Itasca from the axe.

The Minnesota Legislature created Itasca State Park—the state's first—in 1891. "Itasca Lake and its preservation is sacred and dear to every American heart," Governor Knute Nelson said of the new park in 1895.

But it granted lumbermen the right to cut the timber. Brower fought the timber harvesting, appealing both to the industry's barons as well as Minnesota's political leaders. "Rescue or continued destruction. Which?" Brower asked in a volume about the park published by the Minnesota Historical Society in 1904. The destruction continued. The forests around Lake Itasca—except the lake's northwest shore—were cut even as the new park was created. Even so, today, the park is one of the state's most popular, with nearly 500,000 visitors in 2008.

### Lesson 1—Understand a watershed

A watershed is the area of land where all of the water that is on or under it drains into the same place. It is an important

As we manage the river for industry and recreation, so is it necessary for our management of the river's ecological health.

The health of our water depends upon what we do on the land.

"Water is H2O, hydrogen two parts, oxygen one, but there is also a third thing that makes water and nobody knows what that is."

—D. H. Lawrence

concept for understanding how water bodies are managed. John Wesley Powell, the explorer of the Grand Canyon and later head of the U.S. Geologic Survey, defined watersheds as:

"...that area of land, a bounded hydrologic system, within which all living things are inextricably linked by their common water course and where, as humans settled, simple logic demanded that they become part of a community."

A watershed is delineated on a U.S. Geological Survey topographic map using the blue hydrographic lines symbolizing water and the brown elevation contour lines indicating areas of equal height above sea level. Since water flows downhill from higher elevations to a common body of water, to delineate the watershed boundary for a particular place on a stream or lake, you will need to draw a line connecting the highest elevation points surrounding the lake or stream.

Every water body has a watershed, an area of land draining to it. Sucker Creek is a tiny stream that drains lands in southeastern Clearwater County, and itself drains to the Mississippi Headwaters and Lake Bemidji. Move downstream from the headwaters and a succession of watersheds drain to the Mississippi River—Hennepin and LaSalle Creeks, Turtle River, Schoolcraft River, and so on. The Mississippi River is itself a major drainage basin that drains to the Gulf of Mexico. The U.S. Geological Survey has identified approximately 80 major watersheds in Minnesota which drain to the state's five major river basins: the Minnesota, Mississippi, Red, Rainy, and St. Louis, each of which drains to the Gulf of Mexico, Hudson's Bay, or the Great Lakes.

*DOMINIQUE BRAUD*

Common Loon

For the Mississippi Headwaters, the state has delineated the following watersheds:

- Mississippi Headwaters, Lake Itasca to Pokegama Lake
- Leech Lake River
- Pine River
- Mississippi River, Grand Rapids (through Aitkin)
- Mississippi River, Brainerd (Aitkin to Crow Wing River)
- Mississippi River, Sartell (Morrison County to St. Cloud)

*DOUG OHMAN*

The Mississippi Headwaters Board collaborates with many partners such as the Minnesota DNR to provide recreational opportunities for all to enjoy the river.

INDIANS PICKING WILD

Pub. by W.W. Latta.

"The white men was many and we could not hold our own with them. We were like deer. They were like grizzly bears ... We were contented to let things remain as the Great spirit made them. They were not, and would change the rivers ... if they did not suit them."

—*Chief Joseph of the Nez Perce*

Lake Winnibigoshish

# CASS LAKE TO SCHOOLCRAFT PARK

Broad savannas of large lakes and marsh plains define this 80-mile river section. The Mississippi River flows through Cass Lake into Lake Winnibigoshish and finally through an extensive wetland complex, marked by the Mississippi to the north, Leech Lake River to the west, and White Oak Lake to the east. Unique features are the white sands on Lake Winnibigoshish's southeast shore, sedge meadows, and the stands of upland pines.

It is a section of remarkable biological diversity. The visitor can become a citizen scientist here, observing and recording dragonflies, frogs, toads, or phenological occurrences such as when the lakes freeze in the fall and thaw in the spring.

It is also a section that teaches us about other people. This region is the heart of the reservation held by the Leech Lake Band of Ojibwe, and the Mississippi River and its watershed are the heart of these Native

*-1909-*

Americans' culture and history. Treaties signed in the mid-19th century are still important to land managers of the region.

Ice blocks deposited on plains of outwash formed the large lakes of this river section, Cass and Winnibigoshish. As the glacier melted, it left behind plains covered by outwash. These plains underlie this river section's extensive wetlands, which are located between Cass Lake and Winnibigoshish and at the Mississippi's confluence with the Leech Lake River. The lakes were created when ice blocks deposited in the outwash plain melted.

The sedge meadow is a distinctive vegetative community of this river section. This is an open peat land dominated by sedge grasses, with some shrubs. Sedges are similar to grasses, but their stems have triangular edges, compared to the round edges of grasses. Sedges grow in clumps of stems sprouted from a single horizontal runner. Sedge stems build up in large tufts or tussocks from year to year. The resulting mat of grasses is a home for new plants, until the plant is eventually grounded on the bottom. The tussock helps the plant survive changes in water levels by providing buoyancy in high water and sending out water-seeking roots in low water. This community can be seen on the Mississippi, about halfway between Cass and Winnibigoshish lakes. The area is known as Mississippi Meadows. Wild rice flourishes in the shallow parts of this wetland.

The river's channel runs through glacial till, which is soft and subject to erosion. Because of this material, the channel is easily changed. Abandoned river sections look like half moons or partial circles on the map. They

DOUG OHMAN

*NOTE: (R) and (L) represent right and left banks of the river when facing downstream.*

## GENERAL DESCRIPTION of ROUTE

The Mississippi connects lakes Cass and Winnibigoshish, two large lakes formed as giant ice blocks melted on plains created by glaciers 10,000 years ago. These lakes have always been important to the Ojibwe people of northern Minnesota, and today, lie within the boundaries of the Leech Lake Indian Reservation. These are extensive public lands, managed by the U.S. Forest Service as the Chippewa National Forest. The river is gentle, suitable for novice paddlers. The rewards of the paddle are forested shorelines, pine-covered islands, and eagles soaring overhead.

River miles are counted upstream from the Mississippi's confluence with the Ohio River, according to a system developed by the U.S. Army Corps of engineers.

**1264.0-57.4 Cass Lake**
Cass Lake access/rest area; shelter, telephone, drinking water, picnic area, boat access, parking, dock. Norway Beach Rec Area; shelter, telephone, drinking water, picnic area, campground, boat access, showers, swimming, wheelchair accessible. O'Neils Point; watercraft campsite. South Star Island; watercraft campsite. Schram Lake; watercraft campsite. Nushka Group Site; carry-in access, drinking water, shelter, campground.

**1263.4(L) Carry-in access**

**1257.5(R) Knutson Dam Recreation Area**
Portage right 297 yards. The Chippewa National Forest controls the level of Cass Lake at Knutson Dam, and operates a 40-unit campground at the dam site. The Chippewa National Forest maintains three campgrounds and public accesses on Cass Lake's southeastern shore. There are beautiful sand beaches at these sites. Norway Beach offers interpretive programs in the summer.

**1256.8    State Highway 39 bridge**
This is a gentle stretch of river, bordered by mixed hardwood forest. Most of the land is publicly owned; paddlers will see little development past this point. The river leaves the Mississippi Headwaters Board's "Scenic" designation and enters a section managed as "Wild."

**1253.8(R) Third River Bridge and access**
The access is located on the downriver side of the bridge. The riparian landscape now changes from wooded to wetlands.

**1251.5(R) Mississippi Meadows Mile Marker**
The river broadens into an area known as Mississippi Meadows. Ducks and geese use these wetlands for raising young and beginning their fall migration. The pines on the point, jutting off the river's right bank, are more than 100 years old.

**1250.8(R) Lydick Brook Mile Marker**
The confluence of Lydick Brook from the south help create the Mississippi Meadows. The creek's name comes from a homesteading family whose son represented the area in the U.S. Congress. A significant archaeological site was uncovered when part of the Great River Road system was rebuilt in 1995.

**1250.5(R) Meadows Campsite and carry-in access**

**1250.3(R) Smiling Joe's Campsite and carry-in access**
This is a popular launching spot during wild rice harvest late in the summer.

**1247-1233 Lake Winnibigoshish**
The lake's name means "dirty water" Ojibwe, referring to the effect of wind lake's sandy shorelines. Lake Winnibigo or Winnie, is Minnesota's third largest lake. A slight breeze can produce large w across it. *Caution: do not paddle acros Winnibigoshish. Portage from Reese La (see below) by car to the Winnie Dam Recreation Area on the east side of If you must paddle, do so only in war weather and stay within swimming dis of the shore.*

**1247  (R) Reese Landing**
Located on Winnie's western shore, to right as you enter the lake.

**1246.5(L) Governor's Pt. Cmpst. and carry-in a**

**1246  (L) West Winnie Campground**
Located on the lake's western shore, to left as the paddler enters the lake. Water access, drinking water, rest area.

**1236.5(R) Tamarack Point Water Access**

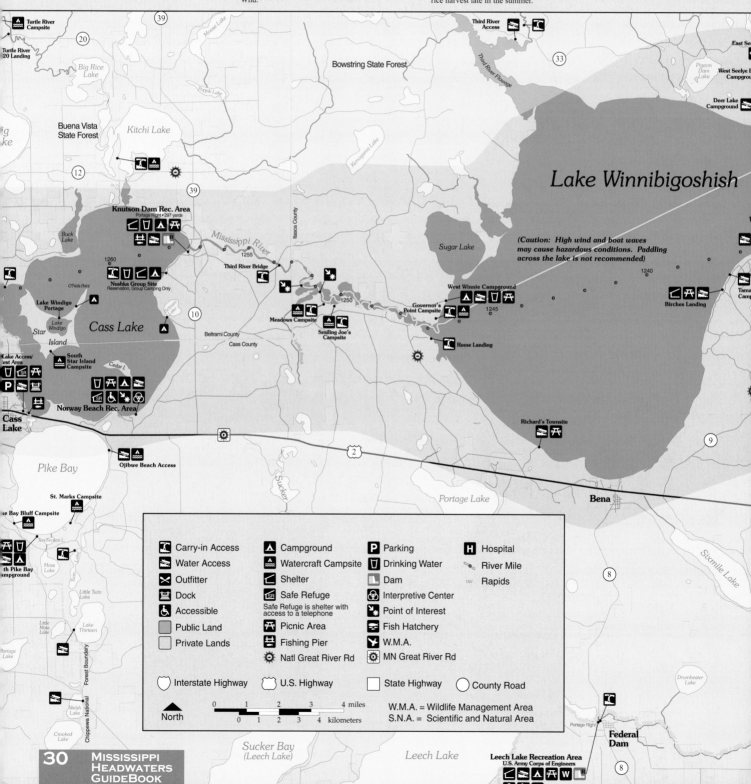

### Map labels

39 · 20 · Turtle River Campsite · Turtle River 20 Landing · Big Rice Lake · Moose Lake · Popple Lake · Bowstring State Forest · Third River Access · 33 · East Se · West Seelye B Campsite · Pigeon Dam Lake · Deer Lake Campground · East Se

Buena Vista State Forest · Kitchi Lake · 12 · 39 · Kenoogining Lake · Lake Winnibigoshish · Sugar Lake · 1240

Knutson Dam Rec. Area · Portage Right • 297 yards · Buck Lake · 1260 · O'Neils Point · Mississippi River · 1255 · Itasca County · Third River Bridge · Nushka Group Site · Reservation, Group Camping Only · Lake Windigo Portage · Lake Windigo · Star · Island · Cass Lake · 10 · Beltrami County · Cass County · 1250 · Meadows Campsite · Smiling Joe's Campsite · Little Brook · West Winnie Campground · Governor's Point Campsite · 1245 · *(Caution: High wind and boat waves may cause hazardous conditions. Paddling across the lake is not recommended)* · Birches Landing · Tama Camp

Lake Access/ est Area · P · South Star Island Campsite · Cedar L. · Norway Beach Rec. Area · Reese Landing · Richard's Townsite · 9

Cass Lake · Pike Bay · Ojibwe Beach Access · Sucker · 2 · Portage Lake · Bena · 8 · Sixmile Lake

St. Marks Campsite · e Bay Bluff Campsite · Ten Section L. · th Pike Bay ampground · Moss Lake · Little Twin Lake · Little Moss Lake · Lake Thirteen · Chippewa National · Forest Boundary · Welch Lake · Crooked Lake · Drumbeater Lake

### Legend

|  |  |
|---|---|
| Carry-in Access | Campground | Parking | Hospital |
| Water Access | Watercraft Campsite | Drinking Water | River Mile |
| Outfitter | Shelter | Dam | Rapids |
| Dock | Safe Refuge | Interpretive Center | |
| Accessible | *Safe Refuge is shelter with access to a telephone* | Point of Interest | |
| Public Land | Picnic Area | Fish Hatchery | |
| Private Lands | Fishing Pier | W.M.A. | |
| | Natl Great River Rd | MN Great River Rd | |

Interstate Highway · U.S. Highway · State Highway · County Road

North · 0 1 2 3 4 miles · 0 1 2 3 4 kilometers

W.M.A. = Wildlife Management Area
S.N.A. = Scientific and Natural Area

Sucker Bay (Leech Lake) · Leech Lake · Leech Lake Recreation Area · U.S. Army Corps of Engineers · Federal Dam · 8

# ILLION RIVER

**Tamarack Pt. Cmpgrd. and carry-in access**
Note: There are several campsites and accesses located on the northeast side of Lake Winnie. See the resource list at the end of this map for contacts.

**Plug Hat Point (L)**

**Winnie Dam Recreation Area**
Portage left 297 yards. The U.S. Congress authorized construction of the dam regulating the level of Lake Winnie in 1881 on lands it had already granted to the Ojibwe people of Minnesota. "No white man knows of the damage that will be done to us," Sturgeon Man, a Lake Winnie resident, told a government commission appointed to address the problem. "Every year what supports us grows on this place. If the dam is built, we will all be scattered, we will have nothing to live on." The dam was built and compensation was provided to Sturgeon Man's ancestors 104 years later, in 1985. The dam elevated water levels about eight feet, wiping out cemeteries, villages, shoreline crops and plants. Today, the Leech Lake Indian

Reservation's fish hatchery is located near the dam site.

**1231.5(L)  Little Winnibigoshish Lake**

**1228.2(L)  Crazy James' Point**
This river access only campsite is located in a mixed pine and hardwood forest.

**1221.5(R)  U.S. Highway 2**
The Mississippi's channel is lined with fine white sands, remnants of a time 6,000 years ago when the landscape was much drier and Lake Winnie was ringed with sand dunes. The Chippewa National Forest now conducts prescribed burns of the wetlands, which has brought back several plant species. If the river level gauge reads 5.0' or above, water is high; water level is medium at 2.0' to 5.0', and water is low below 2.0'.

**1216.5(L)  Leech Lake River Access and campsite**
The Leech Lake River meets the Mississippi here.

**1215  (R)  Gambler's Point campsite and rest area**
This campsite provided the only access to

land from the river as it makes its way though a series of oxbows, created as the river cut channels in soft material laid down by glaciers. Many of these had been dredged during logging years to provide a more direct route for log movement.

**1209.5 & 1208(L)  Channels to White Oak Lake**
From White Oak Lake Access it is a one mile walk to Deer River for supplies.

**1205.2(L)  Little White Oak Lake**
It is a 1.5 mile paddle from the Mississippi River to the Little White Oak Lake Access.

**1201.5(R)  Schoolcraft State Park**
The Vermillion River joins the Mississippi River at Schoolcraft State Park, a small park with a handsome stand of red pine. Camping and public access are available at the park, including two river access only campsites.

This location marks the down river boundary of this map. Refer to map 3, Vermillion River to Palisade for further information.

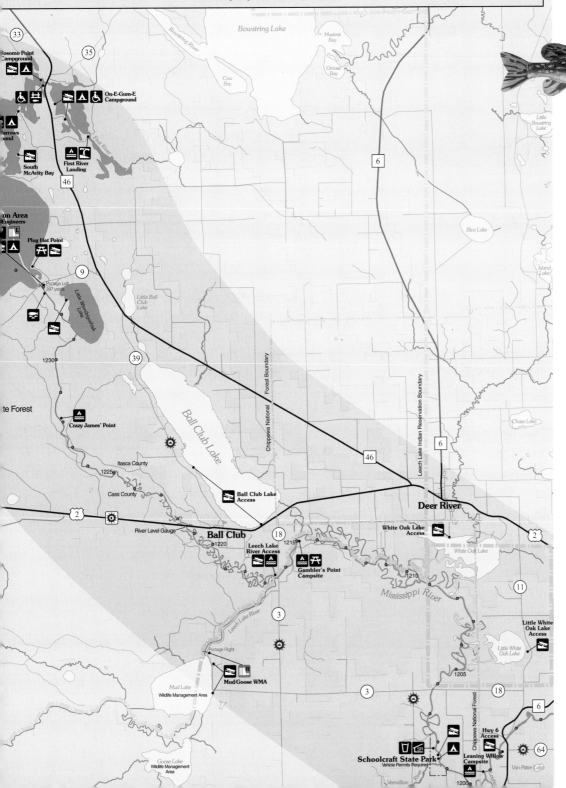

Northern Pike

*DOUG OHMAN*

Exploring the Headwaters of the Mississippi River can be almost as rewarding by land as it is by water.

DOMINIQUE BRAUD

Minnesota has the largest number of breeding bald eagles in the lower 48 states. One-third or more of the state's eagle nests are located in the Chippewa National Forest.

Largemouth Bass

are literally sections of river channel cut off from the main channel as water levels fell, and are filling with vegetation. The oxbows and marshes they lie in are the remains of a braided stream channel created as glacial meltwater rushed downriver thousands of years ago.

Where the Mississippi River leaves Lake Winnibigoshish, the river's bottom is covered in fine white sand. This material literally blew in from the west during a particularly hot and dry period thousands of years ago. A similar formation of white sands is found further downriver, below Brainerd.

The archaeological record shows human habitation on this river section dating to the Paleoindian period following the retreat of the glaciers. Jacob Brower mapped burial mounds—from the Woodland period—at the confluence of the Mississippi and Leech Lake rivers. Village sites were located on the margins of lakes and rivers, especially Lake Winnibigoshish and White Oak Lake. The historic record documents the story of the Dakota who lived here at the time of first European contact, and the Ojibwe people who live here now. The Leech Lake Band of Ojibwe is linked to the Algonquian people, originally from the eastern United States, from whom 27 tribes trace their ancestry, including the Cree, Ottawa, and Potawatomi. The origin of the word Ojibwe has many interpretations, but native speakers prefer to use the definition that is closest to the morphological origins of the word—"he writes."

The Ojibwe were successful and influential participants in the fur trade, which influenced their own expansion and well-being. Both the French and the British sought alliances with the Ojibwe, and the Ojibwe language became the language of the fur trade. Early in the fur trade years, the Dakota and Ojibwe were also friends, forming an alliance that helped the Ojibwe bring the fur trade deep into the North American continent. The relationship was complicated and poisoned by the wars associated with the fur trade in the early part of the 18th century, and later, the conflict between the French, the British, and the Iroquois. The Ojibwe even became pitted against their allies, the Dakota—a brutal period of warfare between the two groups erupted, which continued into the 19th century.

From Lake Superior in the east to the Red River of the North, the Ojibwe and Dakota fought for possession of a region that was resource-rich, providing fish, game, berries, wild rice, and syrup. These skirmishes were recorded by surveyors from the United States government, who often found that one or the other band had torn out the survey stakes. The non-native understands this conflict as the result of the power of the United States extending into new territories; the Ojibwe person understands this conflict as a claim for his people's sovereignty.

Wild rice played a role in these conflicts. Wild rice is a grass, belonging to the family Gramineae, the genus Zizania, and the species aquatica. It is the only cereal native to North America. It grows only in shallow mudbottomed areas with relatively little flow. Its roots

Wild Rice

anchor in muddy bottoms of lakes and rivers, and once established become dense and deep. It is particularly well suited to the Mississippi River, which provides the right combination of muddy bottom and slow, mineral-rich waters. "It grows abundantly ... along the sloughs of the Mississippi River from its headwaters almost as far south as the state of Mississippi; indeed it doubtless occurs along the entire course of this river," Albert Jenks wrote in his 1900 study of the plant. "Nowhere will it grow in water having a sand or clay bed, or in swiftly moving streams," he wrote.

Wild rice was a staple of the diet of the first people and, as the Ojibwe moved into the region, it became an important part of their diet and economy as well. Wild rice sustained people through harsh winters and poor hunting seasons. It was more important to gather and prepare wild rice than to hunt furs to trade with the Europeans. People fought for control of a wild rice lake, and they also kept conflict out of some resource-rich areas so all people could share in the produce.

Treaty rights are a cornerstone of Ojibwe political and cultural identity. Treaties written in the 1850s acknowledged the sovereignty of the tribes and the federal government's role as trustee of that sovereignty. Members of the Leech Lake Band point out that they have been dealing with the federal government longer than Minnesota has been a state.

Ojibwe people at Lake Winnibigoshish and Leech Lake asserted their treaty rights in the 1880s, when the U.S. Army Corps of Engineers was authorized to begin construction of dams to manipulate water levels on the lakes to benefit lumbering and milling at Minneapolis, more than 200 river-miles away.

The dams raised the water levels on Lake Winnibigoshish, which was naturally relatively shallow and one of the more productive wild rice lakes. The higher water levels destroyed much of the wild rice stands.

The dams were to be built on lands that the federal government had acknowledged belonged to the Ojibwe, but the legislation authorizing construction overlooked that fact. The Ojibwe protested the construction, arguing their case before a claims commission meeting in St. Paul.

"No white man knows of the damage that will be done to us. As long as the sun shall pass over our heads we would have been able to live here if this dam had not been commenced. Every year

Knutson Dam on Cass Lake

*DOUG OHMAN*

what supports us grows on this place. If this dam is built we will all be scattered, we will have nothing to live on," the Pillager leader, Sturgeon Man, told the commission.

"No one that comes here and stops for a while can know how important this is to us. When our lands were given to us by the Great Father we could do something, but if these dams are made we will all be destroyed," said Flatmouth, chief of the Pillager band.

The commission recommended compensation and construction proceeded. Despite the commission's findings, the Ojibwe claims for the compensation for taking of the land and damages caused by flooding villages, cemeteries, wild rice beds, were not resolved until 1985, 104 years after the dams became operational.

"Wild rice is the most nutritive single food which the Indians of North America consumed. The Indian diet of this grain, combined with maple sugar, bison, deer, and other meats, was probably richer than that of the average American family of today."
~Albert E. Jenks, 1900

## Community Management 2: Understanding tribal sovereignty

The Leech Lake Band of Ojibwe occupy an area of woods and water in north central Minnesota that is part of the headwaters of the Mississippi River. The original reservation was more than 854,000 acres in size and included the three large lakes of Leech, Cass, and Winnibigoshish, which cover 300,000 acres. The remaining acreage is the heart of Minnesota's lakes country, with some of the land once held in trust for the band now owned by seasonal visitors, as second homes or resorts.

The governing structure for the Leech Lake Reservation and its communities is established through the constitution of the Minnesota Chippewa Tribe. The 1934 Indian Reorganization Act vested this authority in the Minnesota Chippewa Tribe. The Minnesota Chippewa Tribe includes the reservations located at Bois Forte, Fond du Lac, Grand Portage, Leech Lake, Mille Lacs, and White Earth. A five-member Reservation Business Committee governs each reservation.

Operation of the reservation's three casinos and bingo operations are directed through the Leech Lake Gaming Division. Leech Lake, like the other Minnesota Chippewa bands with gaming, entered into a perpetual compact with the state of Minnesota to provide slot machines and blackjack gambling.

The chairman and secretary-treasurer of each of the six Chippewa reservations serve on the Tribal Executive Committee of the Minnesota Chippewa Tribe. The Minnesota Chippewa Tribe's executive director is responsible for the daily operation of all tribal affairs, including intergovernmental relations, the performance of staff, and the achievement of goals by

Painted Turtle

• On one gallon of fuel, 1 ton of cargo can be moved 60 miles by truck, 202 miles by rail, and 514 miles by barge.

• One barge holds as much as 15 jumbo rail hoppers and 58 semi truck trailers.

• One bargeload of wheat is enough to bake 2.25 million loaves of bread.

DOUG OHMAN

NATURAL RESOURCE MANAGEMENT
ON THE
LEECH LAKE INDIAN RESERVATION

DIVISION OF RESOURCE MANAGEMENT
LEECH LAKE RESERVATION BUSINESS COMMITTEE

programs administered by the Minnesota Chippewa Tribe. The executive director assists tribal leadership by identifying and developing policy objectives and then implementing policy once the Tribal Executive Committee adopts it. The executive director also administers daily operation of all tribal programs and services.

*DOMINIQUE BRAUD*

Great Grey Owl

The Leech Lake Band of Ojibwe has adopted rules for lands on the Mississippi River or Headwaters lakes held in fee or trust by enrolled members of the Minnesota Chippewa Tribe. The band is a sovereign government, so administration of similar rules by the band and the four Mississippi Headwaters counties lying within the reservations boundary, is unique.

### Lesson 2—Be a citizen scientist

Citizen scientists can be defined two ways: first, as individuals who are interested in contributing scientific information but are not formally trained as scientists. The second definition is people who are trained as scientists, who want to build a better understanding of the resource, and who understand that their work as scientists is part of a broader context that includes consideration of related political, social, and economic issues. Monitoring parts of the river's setting brings the two together and provides information that can improve decision-making.

Monitoring is the periodic or continuous collection of data using consistent methods. The methods are developed by a credible program and grounded in current scientific knowledge and practice. Volunteer monitors are trained in collection or observation methods and follow a common protocol in making and reporting measurements.

The National Audubon Society's Annual Christmas Bird Count has been organizing volunteers to count birds at holiday time for more than 100 years. The long-term data has enabled scientists to measure trends in bird populations and make recommendations for bird conservation. There is a Mississippi Headwaters Audubon Society chapter based in Bemidji that participates in the national project. http://birds.audubon.org/get-involved-christmas-bird-count/

River Watch and other community-based volunteer programs have been established by the Mississippi Headwaters Board to collect and monitor the river's vital signs.

Other national bird survey programs are Project Feeder Watch and the breeding bird survey. http://birds.cornell.edu/citscitoolkit/features/learning-network-for-citizen-science-and-conservation

Many volunteer monitoring or citizen science programs measure aspects of climate or seasonal change, known as phenology. The Minnesota Climatology Work Group depends on volunteers to measure rainfall at rain gauges and to report ice-on and ice-out dates on lakes. http://climate.umn.edu/doc/ice_out/ice_out_status_10.html

Another project asks volunteers to report when certain plants bud in the spring, including lilacs and red osier dogwood, which are found in the Mississippi Headwaters region. Phenological observations have been used for centuries by farmers to maximize crop production, by nature-lovers to anticipate optimal wildflower viewing conditions, and by almost all of us to prepare for seasonal allergies. Today scientists are using reports of budding to track the effect of climate on organisms and to make predictions about the future health of the environment. http://neoninc.org/budburst/

The presence of dragonflies and damselflies indicate good water quality in lakes and streams. These insects live for several years on river and lake bottoms in their nymph stage, hatch, and spend only a day or so as adults. The Minnesota Odonata Survey recruits volunteers to record their observations.   www.mndragonfly.org/

The presence of frogs and toads also indicate healthy biological conditions. The Minnesota DNR organizes the MN Frog and Toad Calling Survey. Volunteers are given routes to drive over several dates in spring and early summer and asked

*CHIP BORKENHAGEN*

Pasque Flower

Spring Peeper

to listen for frog and toad songs. A record of frog calls helps them identify the species they are hearing. This project connects to a national amphibian-monitoring project coordinated by the U.S. Geological Survey. dnr.state.mn.us/volunteering/frogtoad_survey/index.html

www.pwrc.usgs.gov/naamp/

*• The Upper Mississippi is host to more than 50 species of mammals.*

*• At least 145 species of amphibians and reptiles inhabit the Upper Mississippi River environs.*

Leopard Frog

"The richest value of wilderness lie not in the days of Daniel Boone,
nor even in the present but rather in the future.
The good life on any river may...depend on the perception of its
music, and the preservation of some music to perceive."

*—Aldo Leopold*

*CROW WING COUNTY HISTORICAL SOCIETY*

(From the back of the photo) "Bug-ah-na-ge-shig, commonly known as 'Bug', can rightly bear claim to the title of 'the only unconquered Indian in the United States'...Walker, Minnesota, April 7, 1899, at Boy Lake on the Leech Lake reservation."
Pictured are Chief Red Hair, his wife, Bug-ah-na-ge-shig, and Go-ne-wah-quod.

People have lived in the Mississippi Headwaters for nearly 10,000 years. Here is a glimps of the previous periods of this region:

**Paleoindian:** dating from 5,000 to 8,000 years ago, these people were seasonal inhabitants of the region, whose livelihood depended on hunting big game, and are known to us by their stone tools.

**Archaic:** dating from 2,000 to 5,000 years ago, these people were hunters and gatherers, who used a variety of resources including wild rice, fish and game, and practiced social and spiritual organization. They are also know to us by their pottery, burial mounds, trails, habitation and work sites.

**Woodland:** dating from modern to 2,000 years ago, these people established villages, and had specific sites for hunting, processing of fish and animal foods, maple sugar and wild rice. They are known to us by the evidence of their villages, tools and the oral traditions of the Dakota and Ojibwe people.

**Pre-settlement:** contact with Europeans in the Mississippi Headwaters region was established in the 17th and 18th centuries, during the original white exploration and fur trade. Pressure of white settlement of the region became more intense in the mid-19th century, resulting in the forced re-location of the native people onto reservations.

"These falls are a lovely prelude to the Falls of St. Anthony, five hundred miles downstream. They have the additional advantage of giving the traveler the sensation one feels only in mountains, this in a region where there are none. One's imagination, dulled by a monotonous and tiring navigation over so many slow winding rivers, is enlivened by the sight of impetuous torrent."

—Joseph Nicollet, 1836

Dam originally built as Blandin Paper Company power station - now owned by UPM. This is the site of the falls referenced by Joseph Nicol

# SCHOOLCRAFT PARK TO PALISADE

In this 80-mile river section, the Mississippi River flows east from the lands of Leech Lake Reservation and the Chippewa National Forest through the city of Grand Rapids and then turns south, where it twists and turns across a deep bed of clay and sand deposited by glaciers thousands of years ago. This region inspires the visitor to imagine long-gone scenes: how the river once tumbled over the rocks that gave the town its name and how great sheets of ice built a mountain in one part and flattened the landscape in another. In this section the Mississippi River touches two of Minnesota's three biological communities: the pine or conifer forests of the north and the mixed hardwoods of the east and central part of the state. These forests built and sustain much of the region's economy even today.

The town of Grand Rapids got its name, more than a century ago, from the falls, or series of rapids, that started at the current location of Pokegama Dam and stepped down over a series of rock shelves, dropping nine feet over two miles. The Mississippi was dammed at Pokegama Falls in the late 19th century, as part of the improvements ordered by the U.S. Congress that included dams at the outlet of Lake Winnibigoshish and Leech Lake. The second dam, located at the bottom of these rapids, still provides power for the paper company founded by Charles Blandin.

Because the dams were built by the federal government, they had to serve a public purpose. The U.S. Army Corps of Engineers determined that purpose was to aid navigation downstream at Minneapolis and St. Paul. Construction of the dams was opposed by the Ojibwe people whose lands were flooded by the dams on what had been relatively shallow lakes. In the early years of the 20th century, the dams were the source of controversy for people living in the downstream end of this river section.

A good place to imagine what the river once looked like is Portage Park, or the Bass Brook Wildlife Management Area, which can be reached by turning south on Itasca County 63, from US Highway 2, west of Grand Rapids. The town of Cohasset manages Portage Park and the state of Minnesota manages Bass Brook Wildlife Management Area. The latter is a 300 acre preserve with a Great Blue Heron rookery, nesting bald eagles and a variety of other birds. The falls are flooded, but 15-foot quartzite cliffs rise above the river. Most of the region's ancient bedrock is buried under materials left by glaciers; this bedrock is part of the formation that extends northeasterly towards the Iron Range and Lake Superior, and is the only exposed bedrock in the Mississippi Headwaters.

The giant ice sheet that covered northern Minnesota advanced from different directions over thousands of years. It is possible to see how glaciers moved in this river section. These advances are called "lobes."

From the northwest and west, one lobe from the ice sheet deposited piles of dirt and rocks that created the rugged terrain known as Sugar Hills. Big Thunder Peak is the tallest of these hills, rising to more than 1,700 feet above sea level. It is part of a large parcel owned by Rajala Lumber Company but managed cooperatively as a Minnesota Forest Legacy Area. The timber will be harvested, but the lands are open for recreational uses including hunting, cross country skiing and snowmobiling. The Sugar Hills Forest Legacy Area is located south of Grand Rapids, west of Highway 169 and accessed by Itasca County Road 449.

"Blue Flag" Iris

DOUG OHMAN

# ROUTE DESCRIPTION • VERMILLION RIVER TO PALISADE

*NOTE: (R) and (L) represent right and left banks of the river when facing downstream.*

## GENERAL DESCRIPTION of ROUTE

This river section is located about 200 river miles downstream of Lake Itasca and about 300 river miles upstream of Minneapolis–St. Paul.

Paddling is easy, but is interrupted by two dams, one controlling the level of Lake Pokegama and the other providing hydropower to Blandin Paper Company. Both must be portaged.

This is a section of transition, from the wetlands and forests of the Chippewa National Forest though the town of Grand Rapids, to the lowland hardwood forest of Aitkin County. The town of Grand Rapids is growing, from the Minnesota Power generating facility west of town to the confluence with the Prairie River east of town. The river runs south downstream of Grand Rapids, and the shorelines become agricultural and the forested, as it meanders into Aitkin County. River miles are counted upstream from the Mississippi's confluence with the Ohio River, according to a system developed by the U.S. Army Corps of Engineers.

sites dating to Dakota occupations more than 3,000 years ago, a heron rookery and large wetland. It is a popular spot for observing bird migration.

**1187 (L) Pokegama Lake Recreation Area/Dam**
It is a 44 yard portage around Pokegama Dam. The dam is operated by the U.S. Army Corps of Engineers to enhance a variety of water uses, such as wild rice crops above the dam, fish spawning in the spring and fall, and to protect private property on Lake Pokegama.

**1185.8(R) Izaak Walton Park**
It was developed by the local chapter of the Izaak Walton League. Its a great way to get on the Mississippi River above the Blandin Paper Mill, a river stretch known locally as the "Mill Pond."

**1185.3(R) Minnesota Forest History Center**
It's Wanagan Landing recreates lumbering days of 100 years ago.

**1184.5(R) Sylvan Municipal Park Access**

**1183.6(R) Blandin Paper Company Dam**
The Mill Pond reservoir ends at the Blandin Paper Company Dam. The dam must be portaged right. 1200 yards. Blandin Paper Company has provided southeasterly through a mixed hardwood-conifer

**1144 (R) Jacobson Campground**
Just above the Swan River confluence, Aitkin County maintains a popular campground and access point. The county also maintains a wayside rest on the right bank, below the campsite but just above the bridge. The town of Jacobson is building a recreation center on the left bank, above the bridge.

**1141.3(R) Jacobson Wayside Rest**
Located before State Highway 200 bridge. Stop for supplies in town which is on the left side of the river. The steamer "Fawn Lake" sank at this location in 1894.

**1132 (R) Willow Wood Campsite**
River access only.

**1126.7 Powerline crossing**

**1126 (L) Ms. Keto Campsite**
River access only. Watch for riffles and rocks at low river conditions in this river section.

**1121.9 (L)Two River Springs**
This state-designated trout stream drains to the Mississippi from the east.

**1121.6**   Bargoline campion

## Legend

| | |
|---|---|
| Carry-in Access | Campground |
| Water Access | Watercraft Campsite |
| Outfitter | Shelter |
| Dock | Safe Refuge |
| Accessible | |
| Public Land | Picnic Area |
| Private Lands | Fishing Pier |
| | Natl Great River Rd |

Safe Refuge is shelter with access to a telephone

| | |
|---|---|
| Hospital | Parking |
| Dam | Drinking Water |
| Interpretive Center | Point of Interest |
| Fish Hatchery | W.M.A. |
| River Mile | MN Great River Rd |
| Rapids | |

| | |
|---|---|
| Interstate Highway | State Highway |
| U.S. Highway | County Road |

W.M.A. = Wildlife Management Area
S.N.A. = Scientific and Natural Area

0   1   2   3   4 miles
0   1   2   3   4 kilometers

North

**1201.8(L) Schoolcraft State Park**
The Vermillion River flows northeasterly from conifer swamp lands lying in the Chippewa National Forest. From there, the Mississippi flows

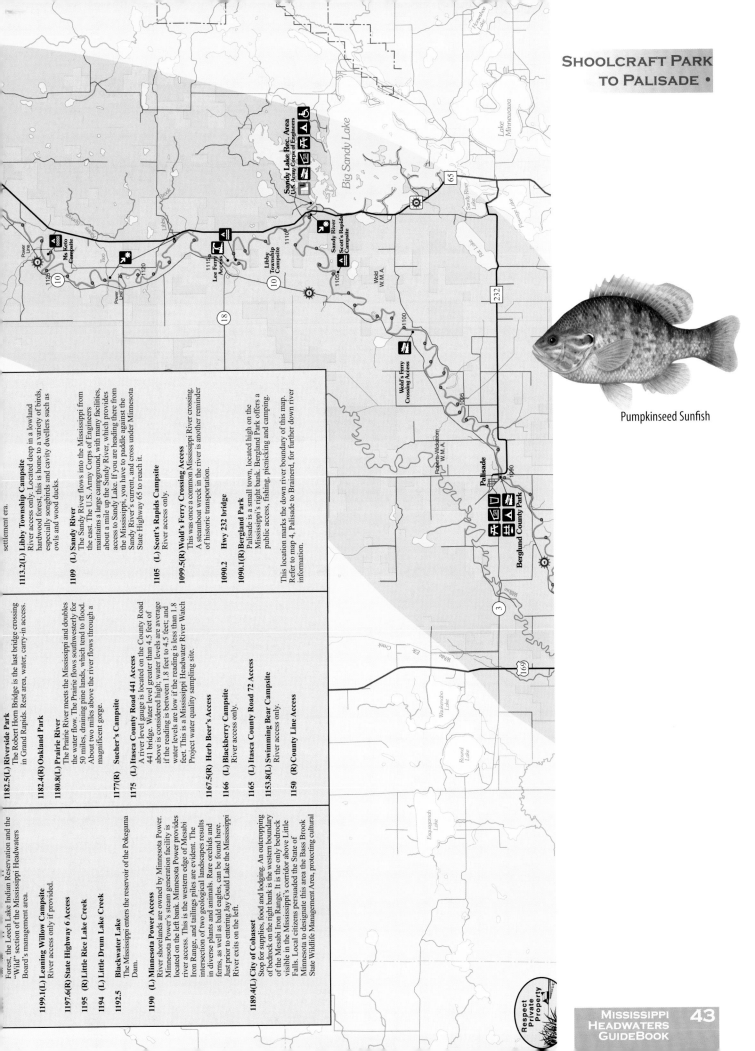

Pumpkinseed Sunfish

Forest, the Leech Lake Indian Reservation and the "Wild" section of the Mississippi Headwaters Board's management area.

**1199.1(L) Leaning Willow Campsite**
River access only if provided.

**1197.6(R) State Highway 6 Access**

**1195   (R) Little Rice Lake Creek**

**1194   (L) Little Drum Lake Creek**

**1192.5      Blackwater Lake**
The Mississippi enters the reservoir of the Pokegama Dam.

**1190   (L) Minnesota Power Access**
River shorelands are owned by Minnesota Power. Minnesota Power's steam generation facility is located on the left bank. Minnesota Power provides river access. This is the western edge of Mesabi Iron Range, and tailings piles are evident. The intersection of two geological landscapes results in diverse plants and animals. Rare orchids and ferns, as well as bald eagles, can be found here. Just prior to entering Jay Gould Lake the Mississippi River exits on the left.

**1189.4(L) City of Cohasset**
Stop for supplies, food and lodging. An outcropping of bedrock on the right bank is the western boundary of the Mesabi Iron Range. It is the only bedrock visible in the Mississippi's corridor above Little Falls. Local citizens persuaded the State of Minnesota to designate this area the Bass Brook State Wildlife Management Area, protecting cultural

settlement era.

**1182.5(L) Riverside Park**
The Robert Horn Bridge is the last bridge crossing in Grand Rapids. Rest area, water, carry-in access.

**1182.4(R) Oakland Park**

**1180.8(L) Prairie River**
The Prairie River meets the Mississippi and doubles the water flow. The Prairie flows southwesterly for 50 miles, draining pine lands, which tend to flood. About two miles above the river flows through a magnificent gorge.

**1177(R)   Sucher's Campsite**

**1175   (L) Itasca County Road 441 Access**
A river level gauge is located on the County Road 441 bridge. Water level greater than 4.5 feet above is considered high; water levels are average if the reading is between 1.8 feet to 4.5 feet; and water levels are low if the reading is less than 1.8 feet. This is a Mississippi Headwater River Watch Project water quality sampling site.

**1167.5(R) Herb Beer's Access**

**1166   (L) Blackberry Campsite**
River access only.

**1165   (L) Itasca County Road 72 Access**

**1153.8(L) Swimming Bear Campsite**
River access only.

**1150   (R) County Line Access**

**1113.2(L) Libby Township Campsite**
River access only. Located deep in a lowland hardwood forest, this is home to a variety of birds, especially songbirds and cavity dwellers such as owls and wood ducks.

**1109      Sandy River**
The Sandy River flows into the Mississippi from the east. The U.S. Army Corps of Engineers maintains a large campground, with many facilities, about a mile up the Sandy River, which provides access to Sandy Lake. If you are heading there from the Mississippi, you have to paddle against the Sandy River's current, and cross under Minnesota State Highway 65 to reach it.

**1105   (L) Scott's Rapids Campsite**
River access only.

**1099.5(R) Wold's Ferry Crossing Access**
This was once a common Mississippi River crossing. A steamboat wreck in the river is another reminder of historic transportation.

**1090.2      Hwy 232 bridge**

**1090.1(R) Berglund Park**
Palisade is a small town, located high on the Mississippi's right bank. Bergland Park offers a public access, fishing, picnicking and camping.

This location marks the down river boundary of this map. Refer to map 4, Palisade to Brainerd, for further down river information.

Sandy Lake Rec. Area
(U.S. Army Corps of Engineers)

Big Sandy Lake

Ms Keto Campsite

Lee Ferry Access

Libby Township Campsite

Sandy River

Scott's Rapids Campsite

Wold W.M.A.

Wold's Ferry Crossing Access

Roberts-Wickstrom W.M.A.

Palisade

Berglund County Park

Respect Private Property

"When you put your hand in a flowing stream, you touch the last that has gone before and the first of what is still to come.
In time and with water, everything changes. Water is the driver of Nature."

—*Leonardo da Vinci*

Another glacial lobe moved west and southwest from the Lake Superior basin. Its path is marked by outwash and flat plains that were once two glacial lakes. Glacial lakes were created when meltwater was dammed by iceblocks or other material. Glacial Lake Upham drained to the northeast, eventually meeting the St. Louis River. One can see the broad flat wetlands as you travel east towards Floodwood and Warba on US Highway 2 from Grand Rapids.

Follow the Mississippi River south on Itasca County 3, the Great River Road, towards Jacobson, and there turn south on Highway 65, to see the terrain created by Glacial Lake Aitkin. Savanna State Forest and Savanna Portage State Park are named for the grassy meadows that covered this outwash plain. East of the park, the water flows to Lake Superior. West of the park, the water flows to the Mississippi. The Savanna Portage was the passage for Native Americans, fur traders and missionaries from Lake Superior and the Great Lakes to the Mississippi River, the Red River of the North and the Great Plains.

This river section represents a crossroads from Lake Superior to the northeast, the St. Louis River and the Mississippi River. Aboriginal people, fur traders, explorers and loggers, all negotiated the boggy lands of the Savannah Portage, from the St. Louis River to Sandy Lake. It took Henry Schoolcraft's expedition 10 days to travel the portage in July 1832. The "route was of the worst character," wrote Lieutenant James Allen, as the travelers slogged through "deep, ugly swamps."

The mixed hardwood-conifer forest is a distinctive vegetative community of this river section. Both species – the hardwood and the softwood – dominate in this forest. Tree species include red, white and jack pines, quaking aspen, big-toothed aspen, paper birches and oaks.

The soils of the mixed hardwood-conifer forest are moist and rich in nutrients. The forest has a variety of plant life, wildflowers and herbs on the floor, and shrubs that grow above it. The life and decay of these plants, together with the litter from the trees, continually builds the nutrients of the soils.

Sunlight helps sustain the diversity of this mixed hardwood-conifer forest. In spring, when the tree canopy is sparse, sunlight floods the forest floor and wildflowers bloom. As the canopy leafs out, the sunlight diminishes and shade-loving plants grow below. A fallen tree creates an opening for sunlight that enables new growth of sun-loving trees and plants.

White and red pines are distinctive trees of the sandy-soiled uplands. These pines are long-lived, straight and grow to great heights. These pines were the focus of the nation's logging industry, which followed the white pine's habitat, from the northeastern tip of Maine across the Great Lakes to Minnesota. For 50 years, from after the Civil War to the end of the First World War, logging dominated this river section. Lumbermen used the Mississippi River to move the logs. Steamboats chugged up and down the river, bringing workers to camp, and supplies to farmsteads. There were 79 farmsteads between Aitkin and Jacobson – first known as Mississippi Landing where the steamboats stopped. For those who came by land, but needed to cross the river, riverside dwellers operated ferries. One crossing point was at Ball Bluff where the farmer had erected a system of ropes to pull freight from one side of the river to the other.

Scientists estimate that Minnesota had 31 million acres of pine forest before European settlement; today, the state's pine forest cover 18 million acres. Logging started in the St. Croix River Valley, in the 1830s, and moved west and north over the next 80 years. From 1900 to 1910, the state's sawmills cut two billion board feet of lumber each year, from more than 40 million cords of trees.

*DOMINIQUE BRAUD*

Hairy Woodpecker

*CROW WING COUNTY HISTORICAL SOCIETY*

Lumbering began to decline in 1910, and the timber industry eventually switched from logs to pulp and paper products. In less than 100 years, 68 billion board feet of timber was cut in Minnesota. Today, forestry and related products remain a significant part of the state's economy. The counties of the Mississippi Headwaters are national leaders in developing sustainable or "green" forestry practices and managing forests for ecological as well as economic values. The visitor can explore Min-

nesota's forest history and today's sustainable forest at the Forest History Center, just south of the Mississippi River near Grand Rapids. The site is run by the Minnesota Historical Society.

The dams in Grand Rapids provided hydropower for logging and paper-making enterprises. The forests provided shelter, sustenance, and commerce. The communities of this river section are committed to using the natural resources so that their children and grandchildren can enjoy the same woods and waters that provided for their parents.

### What communities do: Managing timber harvesting and river protection

Forestry is an important economic activity in this river section. Forestry isn't just harvesting trees: it also provides lands for recreation and ecological services, such as absorbing stormwater and taking up nutrients in the roots. Clearwater, Beltrami, Hubbard, Cass, Itasca, Aitkin and Crow Wing counties are among Minnesota's counties managing tax forfeited lands, which were granted to the local units by the state more than 100 years ago.

The counties have long-range plans that guide foresters in making decisions today that will create healthy forests in the next century. These plans balance harvest, especially aspen, with maintaining diverse forests, providing recreation, aesthetics, habitat and water quality. Most of the counties' forest management practices have met the standards and been certified by the International Forest Stewardship Council. Aitkin County was one of the first to seek the certification, which was awarded in 1997. The certification means that the management of Aitkin County's tax forfeited lands meets the social, economic, ecological, cul-

"Believe me, my young friend, there is nothing—absolutely nothing—half so much worth doing as simply messing about in boats. Look here! If you've really nothing else on hand this morning, suppose we drop down to the river together, and have a long day of it?"

—Kenneth Grahame, *The Wind in the Willows*

*DOUG OHMAN*

tural and spiritual needs of present and future generations. To achieve and maintain the certification, the county's land department:

- Follows all applicable laws
- Demonstrates long-term land tenure and use right
- Respects rights of workers and indigenous people
- Provides equitable use and sharing of benefits
- Reduces environmental impact of logging activities
- Identifies areas that need special protection (e.g. cultural or sacred sites, habitat of endangered animals or plants)

Libby Forest is an example of how Aitkin County protects a high conservation value forest. This forest is located on the Mississippi River corridor and is managed to protect the movement of wildlife along the river. Specific management practices encouraged trees of many ages and winter harvest. This forest is located west of Big Sandy Lake, near the Mississippi River in the northeast part of the county.

**Lesson 3 – How to protect the shoreline**

The shape of river channel changes over time, and the conditions of the Mississippi River make this especially true in this river section. The most simple, inexpensive, and valuable form of streambank stabilization is the preservation and restoration of native riparian and floodplain vegetation.

Vegetation, in addition to natural materials and structures, are rudiments of the natural channel design approach that naturally stabilize and protect streambanks. Larger materials such as logs and root wads provide strength and structure and gradually decompose giving streambanks time to re-vegetate and stabilize. For channels to be stable over the long term they need the flexibility to slowly shift with time, which is what native vege-

"As the word Abraham means the father of a great multitude of men, so the word Mississippi means the father of a great multitude of waters. His tribes stream in from east and west, exceedingly fruitful the lands they enrich. In this granary of a continent, this basin of the Mississippi, will not the nations be greatly multiplied and blest?"

—Herman Melville

DOUG OHMAN

"…but as it is I am only a ferryman and it is my task to take people across this river. I have taken thousands of people across and to all of them my river has been nothing but a hindrance on their journey. They have traveled for money and business, to weddings and on pilgrimages; the river has been in their way and the ferryman was there to take them quickly across the obstacle. However, amongst the thousands there have been a few, four or five, to whom the river was not an obstacle. They heard its voice and listened to it, and the river has become holy to them, as it has to me."

—Hermann Hesse, Siddhartha

tation provides. There are many benefits provided by riparian vegetation:

- The roots of riparian vegetation strengthen stream banks and soils;
- Plants remove moisture and nutrients from the soil, creating resistance to erosion and slumping;
- Exposed roots create "roughness" on river banks which reduces the erosive force of water on the banks;
- Riparian vegetation shades the stream, cooling the water and provides refuge for aquatic and terrestrial creatures;
- Vegetated floodplains help reduce the power of floods, and are used by some fish for spawn in the spring and for forage and shelter by amphibians, mammals, birds and waterfowl.

Prior to planting native vegetation, non-native and nuisance species must be completely removed and the bank may need to be re-graded if the bank slope is too steep or unstable. Re-vegetation techniques include planting seeds, seedlings/saplings, live cuttings, and shrubs and hydro seeding. Live cuttings are branches cut from readily sprouting tree species, such as black willow or dogwood, preferably from nearby vegetation that is adapted to the site. These species will grow and root quickly, thereby providing im-

mediate soil strength and erosion protection. The seeds, plants, disturbed soil, and bank toe should be protected from runoff and stream flow during the rooting process.

Crow Wing County's Environmental Services has on-line guidance for homeowners designing riparian vegetative buffers to manage unstable shoreline:

http://www.co.crow-wing.mn.us/planning___zoning/docs/Shoreline_Rapid_Assessment_Model.pdf

Minnesota DNR has on-line instructions and other resources for restoring shoreline:

http://www.dnr.state.mn.us/restoreyourshore/index.html

*DOMINIQUE BRAUD*

**White Tail Deer**

*DOUG OHMAN*

"The eye is perpetually searching for something new, and however it may have been with other explorers, I think that we may venture to say, that with us, novelty has been a far more constant or immediate passion than utility. The lightning splintered pine which raises its dead arms amid the living foliage is suited to call forth a remark . . .it is this search for something distinctive or peculiar that gives us an edge to the zeal of discovery."

—Henry Schoolcraft, 1832

# PALISADE TO BRAINERD

This 80-mile river section meanders across the lake plain of Glacial Lake Aitkin, and then parallels the Cuyuna Range, one of Minnesota's three iron ranges, which extends from Aitkin County downstream to Randall, in Morrison County. The Mississippi River flows through hundreds of feet of soft and unconsolidated glacial materials as it snakes across its floodplain. This river section is a great place to paddle—the flow is gentle and the views are inspiring. The character is rural and wildlife abounds.

Here the Mississippi River reminds us that natural processes may trump the best of human plans. The river channel flows on an ancient glacial lake bed, so when rainfall is heavy, the added water will flood the adjacent lands. Problems can be minimized if lands draining to the river, and to the streams that feed it, are managed to trap or buffer excessive flows.

Navigating the Mississippi River here can be tricky. Its meanders have created oxbows, which are loops made by the river. As water levels rise and fall, the river drops sediment at outer curves, which are eventually cut off from the main channel. Some oxbows are large enough to have been named: Maydale and Clark Lagoon lie below Palisade, and White Elk Lagoon is located at the river's confluence with the Willow River.

The oxbows are significant natural features. The oxbows support floodplain hardwood forests that provide food, shelter, and habitat for numerous birds. Some require a large area of forest, such as songbirds, or birds and waterfowl that nest in the cavities of dead trees, such as owls and mergansers. The waters of the oxbow are still, providing a suitable place for northern pike to spawn and muskrats to build houses.

The shrub swamp is a distinctive vegetative community of this river section. Speckled alder, willows, bog birch, and pussy willow shrubs stand 10 to 15 feet tall. Ferns, tall asters, sedges, and wildflowers grow beneath these dense thickets. The soil is a wet muck made up of decomposing plants and animals. There are often rivulets of water streaming through the swamp, and it usually floods in the spring as the winter snows melt. The shrub swamp is rich in nutrients from the decaying matter, and nourished by the oxygen of the moving water beneath.

These shrubby peat lands are very attractive to birds, including the yellow rail. This marsh bird nests on the ground and eats by probing the sedge grasses for insects. It is very small and hard to see, because of its size and its tendency to stay under cover. Its distinctive click-click-click call sounds like the tapping of keys.

Tamarack is a sun-loving conifer species associated with the shrub swamp. It is a deciduous larch and its needles turn a brilliant yellow before dropping in the fall. It is a pioneer species, that is, the first tree species that moves into bogs and swamps. Black spruce is associated with it, as well as balsam fir and white spruce. The tamarack gets its name from the Ojibwe who used its tough wood to make snowshoes. The inner bark is used as a poultice to treat skin disorders. The outer bark and roots were used by aboriginal people to treat arthritis and aches.

Flooding is a natural problem at Aitkin, due to the flat terrain and the town's setting at the confluence of five rivers. In 1905, the river stayed above flood stage for three weeks in June and July and remained high enough through September that crops were not grown and some farms were abandoned. Residents of Aitkin blamed the operation of the dams on the upstream reservoirs at Leech, Winnibigoshish, Pokegama, and Big Sandy Lake. Their cause was championed by businessmen in Duluth, who believed that the reservoir system unfairly benefited Minneapolis businessmen, to the detriment of Duluthians. The Duluth businesses used the newspapers to run a charity

Red Winged Blackbird    *Dominique Braud*

*At its headwaters, the Mississippi is less than 1 foot deep. The river's deepest section is between Governor Nicholls Wharf and Algiers Point in New Orleans where it is 200 feet deep.*

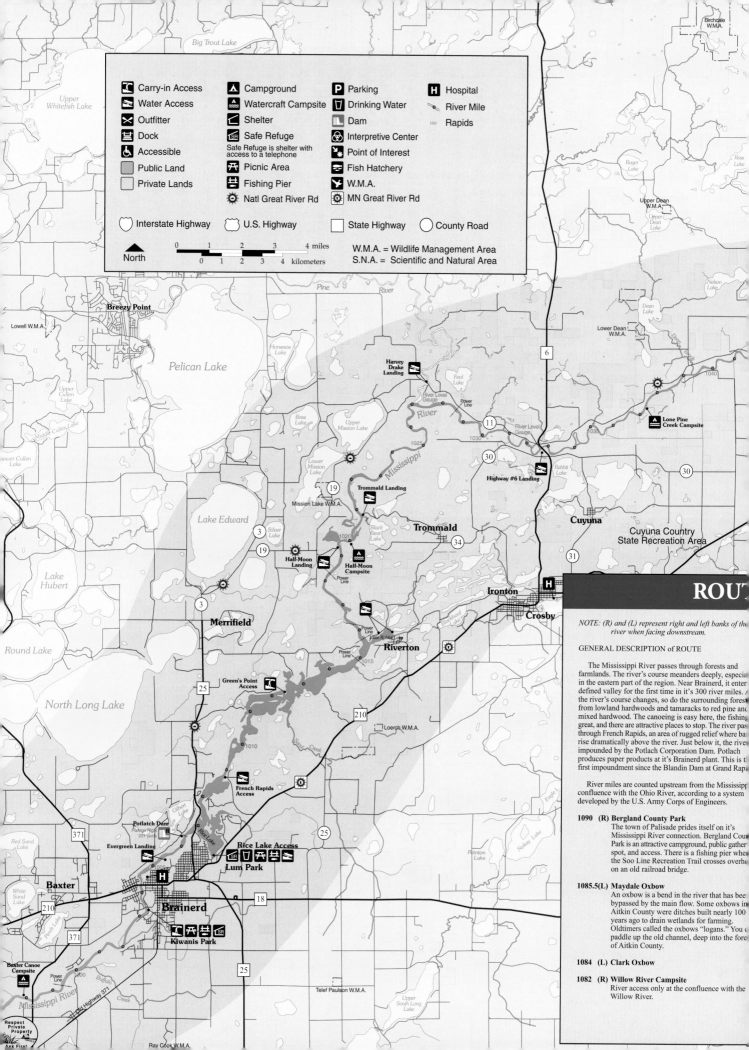

## Legend

- Carry-in Access
- Water Access
- Outfitter
- Dock
- Accessible
- Public Land
- Private Lands
- Campground
- Watercraft Campsite
- Shelter
- SR Safe Refuge
  Safe Refuge is shelter with access to a telephone
- Picnic Area
- Fishing Pier
- Natl Great River Rd
- P Parking
- Drinking Water
- Dam
- Interpretive Center
- Point of Interest
- Fish Hatchery
- W.M.A.
- MN Great River Rd
- H Hospital
- River Mile
- Rapids

Interstate Highway  U.S. Highway  State Highway  County Road

North

0 1 2 3 4 miles
0 1 2 3 4 kilometers

W.M.A. = Wildlife Management Area
S.N.A. = Scientific and Natural Area

## ROUT

NOTE: (R) and (L) represent right and left banks of the river when facing downstream.

GENERAL DESCRIPTION of ROUTE

The Mississippi River passes through forests and farmlands. The river's course meanders deeply, especia[l] in the eastern part of the region. Near Brainerd, it enter[s] defined valley for the first time in it's 300 river miles. A[s] the river's course changes, so do the surrounding forest[s] from lowland hardwoods and tamaracks to red pine and mixed hardwood. The canoeing is easy here, the fishing[is] great, and there are attractive places to stop. The river pas[ses] through French Rapids, an area of rugged relief where ba[nks] rise dramatically above the river. Just below it, the river[is] impounded by the Potlach Corporation Dam. Potlach produces paper products at it's Brainerd plant. This is t[he] first impoundment since the Blandin Dam at Grand Rapi[ds].

River miles are counted upstream from the Mississipp[i] confluence with the Ohio River, according to a system developed by the U.S. Army Corps of Engineers.

**1090 (R) Bergland County Park**
The town of Palisade prides itself on it's Mississippi River connection. Bergland Coun[ty] Park is an attractive campground, public gather[ing] spot, and access. There is a fishing pier whe[re] the Soo Line Recreation Trail crosses overhe[ad] on an old railroad bridge.

**1085.5(L) Maydale Oxbow**
An oxbow is a bend in the river that has bee[n] bypassed by the main flow. Some oxbows in Aitkin County were ditches built nearly 100 years ago to drain wetlands for farming. Oldtimers called the oxbows "logans." You c[an] paddle up the old channel, deep into the fore[st] of Aitkin County.

**1084 (L) Clark Oxbow**

**1082 (R) Willow River Campsite**
River access only at the confluence with the Willow River.

### Map labels

Big Trout Lake
Birchdale W.M.A.
Upper Whitefish Lake
Ross Lake
Upper Dean W.M.A.
Roger Lake
Upper Dean Lake
Lower Dean W.M.A.
Dean Lake
Nelson Lake
Breezy Point
Lowell W.M.A.
Pelican Lake
Pine River
Horsesoe Lake
1040
Upper Cullen Lake
Bass Lake
Upper Mission Lake
Mississippi River
Harvey Drake Landing
Fool Lake
River Level Gauge
Power Line
1025
Lone Pine Creek Campsite
Middle Cullen Lake
Lower Cullen Lake
Lower Mission Lake
Trommald Landing
1030
1035
Rabbit Lake
Highway #6 Landing
Cuyuna
Mission Lake W.M.A.
Lake Edward
Silver Lake
Black Bear Lake
Trommald
Cuyuna Country State Recreation Area
Half-Moon Landing
Half-Moon Campsite
Power Line
Lake Hubert
Ironton
Crosby
Merrifield
Little Robbit Lake
Power Line
Riverton
Blackhood Lake
Round Lake
Power Line
1015
North Long Lake
Green's Point Access
Loerch W.M.A.
1010
Sand Creek
French Rapids Access
Eagle L
Potlatch Dam
Portage Right 201 yards
Gilbert Lake
Rice Lake
Red Sand Lake
Evergreen Landing
Rice Lake Access
Lum Park
1005
Nokay Lake
White Sand Lake
Baxter
Pointon Lake
Brainerd
H
Kiwanis Park
Peach Lake
Upper South Long Lake
Baxter Canoe Campsite
Power Line
1200
Buffalo Creek
Mississippi River
Old Highway 371
Telef Paulson W.M.A.
Ray Cook W.M.A.
Respect Private Property Ask First!

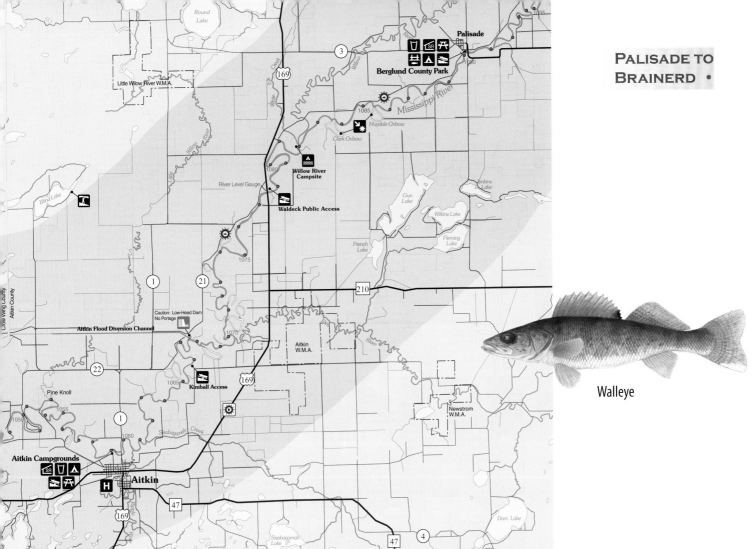

Walleye

# SCRIPTION • PALISADE TO BRAINERD

**Walldeck Public Access**
Located just before U.S. Highway 169. A river level gauge is mounted on the bridge. There are Class I rapids downstream of the access, as well as the low-head dam regulating flow to the Aitkin Diversion Channel. *Caution: When water level is at six feet or more, water will be spilling into the diversion channel located at river mile 1067.5 downriver. Use caution when approaching the dam.*

**Rice River**
The Rice River drains into the 18,000 acre Rice Lake National Wildlife Refuge, managed by the U.S. Fish and Wildlife Service. A 4,500 acre lake there plays an important role in the management of waterfowl. Abundant food, especially wild rice, has attracted people and animals to the site for centuries. The endangered Yellow Rail is found on the refuge.

**Aitkin Flood Diversion Channel**
The dam holds the water in the main river channel during low water. It is the only dam of its type on the Mississippi River. When the water reaches a threatening flood level, it bypasses the main river channel by spilling into the diversion channel. *Use Extreme Caution: Do not approach this dam! It is a low-head dam with hazardous hydraulic conditions on the down river side. Use main river channel only. There is no portage at this dam.*

**Kimball Access**

**Sissabagamah Creek**

**Ripple River**

**Aitkin County Road 1**
The Mississippi at Aitkin captures rivers flowing to it from all four directions; the Willow River from the west, The Rice and Sissabagamah from the east and the Ripple from the south.

**1059 (L) Aitkin Campgrounds and Access**
This is the main stop for the City of Atikin. The downtown area is within walking distance. Stop for supplies, food and lodging. The river steamers Lee, Swan, and Andy Gibson sank in this area. The skeleton of the Andy Gibson is visible at low water. Shelter, telephone and picnic area.

**1053 (R) Pine Knoll**
This homesteading community of Pine Knoll once stood on this spot where the Little Willow River meets the Mississippi River.

**1043.5(R) Aitkin Flood Diversion**
Aitkin Flood Diversion Channel rejoins the river at this point.

**1037.3(L) Lone Pine Creek Campsite**
River access only. No fee, DNR administered.

**1032.8 State Highway 6**
A river level gauge is located on the downstream side of this bridge. Water level is considered high if the gauge reads more than 8.5 feet, and canoers should be cautious in those conditions. Average water levels range between 3.5 and 8.5 feet; water is considered low below 3.5 feet, and boating will be poor when water levels fall to 2 feet or below.

**1032.7(L) Water Access.**

**1028.5 Powerline crossing.**

**1027.1(R) Pine River**
The Harvey Drake landing, one mile up the Pine River, provides water access on the Pine River from Crow Wing County Road 11. The confluence of these rivers is a traditional village site. Native American people lived here first. Lieutenant Zebulon Pike stopped here on his expedition to the Mississippi's Headwaters in December 1805. An Episcopalian mission was built here in the early 19th century.

**1020.8(L) Black Bear Creek & Trommald Landing**
This access is located a short distance up the creek, just below the dam controlling the level of Black Bear Lake.

**1020 (L) Half Moon Campsite**
River access only. No fee, DNR Administered.

**1019.4(R) Half Moon Landing**

**1018.3 - 1016.2 - 1015.8 Powerline crossings.**

**1015.5(L) Little Rabbit Lake Channel**
Access to the Mississippi River is possible at two locations on Little Rabbit Lake at Riverton, on the lake's northwest shore, and on the lake's east shore, about 3/4 mile up lake.

**1014.9 Powerline crossing.**

**1012.5(R) Green's Point Access**
This site is a developed shoreline fishing area. Native American people traditionally camped here during the ricing season in late summer.

**1008.8(L) French Rapids Access**
It is possible to hike beside the river for a mile or two upstream along the bluff. Be prepared; the terrain is steep!

**1006.9(L) Rice Lake Access**
Access is located on the south end of the lake at Brainerd's Lum Park. Drinking water, shelter, picnic area, fishing pier and swimming.

**1006.4 Potlatch Dam**
Portage right 201 yds.

**1005.4(L) Evergreen Landing**

**1003.4(L) Kiwanis Park and Access**
This carry-in access is located at the south end of the City of Brainerd near the Central Lakes College campus. It is a day use park only, with a playground, picnic area, and two fishing piers.

**998.5 Highway 371 bypass bridge**

**998.0 (R) Baxter Campsite**
No fee, DNR administered.

This location marks the down river boundary of this map. Refer to Map 5, Brainerd to Little Falls, for further down river information.

The Mississippi Headwaters Board partners with every governmental agency within its juristiction.

*DOUG OHMAN*

The man-made flood diversion channel eight river-miles north of the city of Aitkin (on Highway 6).

DOUG G.

drive to raise $25,000 for Aitkin County residents flooded that summer.

"The whole river policy, from its inception in building the dam at St. Anthony Falls to the erection of the dams at the outlet of the lakes in the headwaters region, is nothing but a huge and expensive graft worked by adroit, shrewd, scheming men upon the national treasury for their own enrichment," thundered the chairman of the U.S. House of Representatives' Rivers and Harbor Committee. Theodore E. Burton of Ohio, the congressman for the region asked the Corps of Engineers to turn over operation of the dams to the State of Minnesota. Newspapers in Grand Rapids, Deer River, and Walker called for closure of the dams. Others noted that there was little river traffic to actually benefit from the improved navigation in Minneapolis and St. Paul. And, since the railroads charged the same freight rates there as elsewhere, it underscored the point that river navigation did not create competition.

Advocates of the dams pointed out some hard facts—the floods were caused by several complications. For example, some buildings that were flooded were built on areas that were supposed to flood, and their construction was supposed to be prohibited. An exhaustive study of water levels, precipitation, and other measures over the previous 50 years suggested that improper logging practices had made the difference between wet years before and the floods of 1905. It wasn't just that there was more rain, it was that there was no more vegetation in the forests to trap and store rainwater. Without trees to soak up some of the rainwater, almost all of what fell drained directly to streams and rivers, swelling the volume of water beyond the rivers' banks. At this point the streams and rivers of Aitkin County were simply too small to carry all the water that was coming to them. That water had to go someplace, and it rose above banks to the flat fields of the ancient glacial lake plain.

The remedy was not to change the dams: indeed, the Aitkin report showed that the dams had operated to minimize flooding. Since the problem of flooding at Aitkin was perennial, the resulting solution was to build a channel that would divert floodwaters around Aitkin and add another reservoir on the Prairie River, northeast of Big Sandy Lake near the Savanna Portage.

The proposed diversion would have been more than 50 miles, running south, parallel to the Mississippi, from west of Jacobson to Pine Knoll, immediately west of the town of Aitkin. The state drainage engineer said it would cost $150,000 to build. The Corps of Engineers estimated it at more like $1,500,000—a cost that exceeded its public benefit. The ensuing years were dry enough that the idea was shelved. However, wet conditions returned in the 1940s and a much shorter channel was proposed, running just six miles from Hassman to Pine Knoll. This was completed in 1956 for $1,700,000, and it prevented flood damages of twice that amount in its first 20 years of operation.

Below the city of Aitkin, hardwood-covered low banks border the Mississippi River. Sandy bluffs rise 50 feet or more above the river, often opposite broad marshes stretching into the distance. Red and white pines, mixed with oak, birch, and aspen, cover these bluffs. Lying parallel to the river's southern bank is a field of drumlins, hills created as glaciers dropped debris thousands of years ago.

In 1903, homesteader Cuyler Adams noted his compass deflected as he surveyed the land. He guessed it was due to the presence of iron ore, and he was proved right. The Cuyana Range was the third of Minnesota's iron deposits to be discovered and perhaps the only one to be named for a dog— Adams' wife combined the first three letters of her husband's name with the name of their St. Bernard—Una—to name the formation.

Within five years, 2,000 holes had been drilled, seven towns established, and 20 to 30 mines were removing iron ore. The mines flourished through the two World Wars, with the Minnesota iron ranges supplying much of the iron used for military operations. By the 1950s most of the mines closed, leaving many deep abandoned rock stockpiles and mine pits. Two of the towns

remain but the forest has reclaimed most of the town sites. The region is now managed for recreational purposes as the Cuyuna Country State Recreation Area.

At French Rapids, the river is confined to a narrow channel with timbered banks rising more than 100 feet above the water. Steep pine and oak covered hills rise straight out of bogs of ash and maple. Looking towards the river, the hills shade the water. Potholes and ponds dot the inland forest. This is the most rugged area in the headwaters region.

## What communities do: Managing agriculture to protect river quality

The wetlands and marshes of Aitkin County were drained for farming in the 1900s. Many of these projects failed and the land often was forfeited in lieu of paying taxes. Aitkin County has 660 miles of surface ditches that influence water quantity and quality. The drainage ditches can result in additional nutrients and sediment transported to streams and rivers, and they can cause disagreement among neighbors, who may feel they are receiving too much water from an upstream neighbor. Land use activities throughout the watershed can lead to stream instability by changing the amount of water traveling overland. Without the buffer of trees and plants, that water carries more sediment and dirt to the river, which can increase the volume

Young Osprey

*DOMINIQUE BRAUD*

"The mark of a successful man is one that has spent an entire day on the bank of a river without feeling guilty about it."
—*Chinese Proverb*

*DOUG OHMAN*

and velocity of the stream.

Drainage ditches improve agricultural production by moving water from fields early in the planting season. But that changes the natural cycle of water moving from the land to the stream, and can contribute to downstream floods. Plus, the additional load of water erodes away river and channel banks. Again, the channel is too loaded to carry the water and the sediment it picks up. The result is flooding of the lands adjacent to the stream, and enough pressure on the banks to erode and slump off soil into the water.

Ditches can be managed to reduce sediment and to moderate downstream flow. For example, some farmers are building two stages into ditches. The concept is quite simple–the ditch banks are moved back two to three feet from the main channel. The "benches" on either side of the ditch act like a floodplain zone, which enables the high water to spread out, reducing its force or velocity. This practice widens the ditch and also reduces the problems that can occur in ditched areas. Not only does it reduce the volume and velocity of water, but it also improves water quality by minimizing the sediment carried in the floodwater. The system mimics nature to help the farmer prepare fields for early planting, but still minimizes downstream flooding.

Another conservation drainage practice is the installation of a controlled outlet at the mouth of a drainage ditch. This control enables the landowner to stop or reduce the flow of water from the ditch, which reduces the volume and force of the incoming water. In many locations, retaining the water for one or two days reduces the size of downstream floods. In this way, the needs of the farmer and the natural limitations of the flood-prone setting are balanced.

Channel Catfish

### Lesson 4—How to monitor water quality of lakes and streams

Monitoring water quality is at the core of Minnesota's programs to manage its water bodies. Monitoring is the periodic or continuous collection of data of certain parameters, using consistent methods. The types of monitoring and the reasons for collecting data vary tremendously. Water quality monitoring is commonly defined as the sampling and analysis of water (lake, stream, river, or wetland) and conditions of the water body. Water quality monitoring can evaluate the physical, chemical, and biological characteristics of a water body in relation to human health, ecological conditions, and designated water uses.

Some basic reasons for conducting water quality monitoring are to understand current conditions, to measure trends over time, to document seasonal influences, to diagnose issues, or to investigate problems. Minnesota is charged with setting and attaining water quality standards for the state's waters. The state must periodically report to the U.S. Congress the condition of the state's waters. For those waters not meeting state water quality standards, the state must determine the proper pollutant load and how to reach it.

Since the Mississippi Headwaters Board launched River Watch more than 20 years ago, volunteer monitoring has become an integral part of the state's monitoring effort. River Watch was based in high schools and post-secondary institutions along the Mississippi. Students were trained by professionals to collect water quality samples using scientific methods and equipment. Results were used by the state to assess water quality conditions. Minnesota's current water quality monitoring strategy cites citizen or volunteer monitoring as one of four core approaches to monitoring the state's surface waters.

Today, the most popular citizen monitoring program measures clarity of lakes and trans-

Rice Lake, Brainerd

*DOUG OHMAN*

"Sometimes, if you stand on the bottom rail of a bridge and lean over to watch the river slipping slowly away beneath you, you will suddenly know everything there is to be known."
—A. A. Milne, Pooh's Little Instruction Book

parency in streams. Volunteers select sampling sites and, on a regular basis, visit the sites, toss into the water simple black-and-white discs, and lower them into the water until they are no longer visible. That depth is recorded as the limit for clarity or transparency.

A similar device is fitted into the end of a 100-centimeter transparency tube for measuring water quality in streams. When the black-and-white disk disappears at 20 centimeters or less, water quality is considered poor. If it is visible at more than 60 centimeters, water quality is considered good.

Because each stream and lake is unique, the limit to clarity or transparency varies. However, research scientists have used the volunteer data with other measures to define the points at which pollution is actually harming a water body. With more than 10,000 lakes and 90,000 miles of streams, the citizen monitors provide an invaluable service. This simple measure of lake clarity and stream transparency is the foundation of the state's water quality management.

Citizen lake and stream volunteers are also asked to observe the appearance of the water body to evaluate if it is suitable for swimming or boating, assess the effects of recent precipitation, and record the water level for streams. There's a modest cost for materials for entering the program. Learn more at this website:

www.pca.state.mn.us/index.php/water/water-monitoring-and-reporting/volunteer-water-monitoring/volunteer-surface-water-monitoring.html

Smallmouth Bass

(Left) Built in 1910, this bridge carried the Soo Line railroad for 75 years. Now it is an integral part of the Palisade area hiking/biking trail.

(Right) The east end of the diversion channel north of Aitkin in low water conditions (Fall).

"In the time that I have been acquainted with this region I have become increasingly aware of it as a testament of water, the origin and guide of its contours and gradients and of all the lives - the plants and small creatures, and the culture - that evolved here. That was always here to be seen, of course, and the recognition has forced itself, in one form or other, upon people in every part of the world who have been directly involved with the growing of living things.
The gardener who ignores it is soon left with no garden."

—W. S. Merwin, A Shape of Water

# BRAINERD TO LITTLE FALLS

This river section exemplifies the many ways that place shapes people's lives. The prairies on the western edge were hunting grounds for the first people; the river and its tributaries provided transportation, power, and wastewater treatment more recently.

This 80-mile river section runs from the dam below French Rapids, above the town of Brainerd, to the southern border of Morrison County. The Mississippi is a big river here, picking up several rivers from both the western prairies and the hardwood forests of eastern Minnesota. From the west, the streams are Crow Wing, Elk, and Swan. From the east is the Nokasippi. The Crow Wing River flows southeasterly around the glacial end point known as the Itasca moraine, arising in a chain of lakes just east of the Mississippi's headwaters at Lake Itasca. Over the course of geological time, the Mississippi River might cut off its northern channel in favor of this more direct route to the south.

To the west, the Mississippi River is bounded by flat outwash plains covered by sandy soils and prairie vegetation. To the east are hills covered in conifers, maple, and basswood and drained by the Crow Wing River. This river lies in a gap in the morainal system that stretches from Alexandria to Leech Lake and is an ancient natural route to the Red River of the North and the Dakota prairies.

This river section is literally the crossroads of Minnesota's three biological communities—the prairies, the north's pine forests, and the hardwood forest of the east. The Mississippi picks up a major tributary when the Crow Wing River joins it south of Brainerd, and it assumes the width and volume sufficient to provide drinking water to St. Cloud and the Twin Cities.

This river section is also a crossroads for the people and cultures of the region. The prairies and plains attracted large grazing animals—bison, elk, and deer—which were an important food source for Native Americans and the first whites. The earliest cultures depended heavily on hunting. For later cultures, meat was an important part of their diet and economy, but people also gathered wild rice and maple syrup. The entire region can be thought of as an ancient supermarket. Because it was so important for food and survival, the Dakota and the Ojibwe kept hostilities away from the hunting and gathering areas.

For loggers, the river was a way to get logs downriver to the mills in Minneapolis. The first log "drive" down the river was recorded in 1834. For developers, the river represented multiple opportunities. Trading posts on the rivers took advantage of trade and later annuities for the Ojibwe people living at communities in the area. The largest of these was at Ripley, first on the east side of the Mississippi and later on the west side.

The first white residents often operated ferries. For example, William Aitkin was a Scottish fur trader who retired to a spot where the Mississippi River joins the Swan River. He operated a ferry for those who needed to cross the river. Dozens of other landings offered ferry service well into the 20th century.

DOMINIQUE BRAUD

**River Otter**

*The elevation of the Mississippi at Lake Itasca is 1,475 feet above sea level. It drops to sea level at the Gulf of Mexico. More than half of that drop in elevation occurs within the state of Minnesota.*

DOUG OHMAN

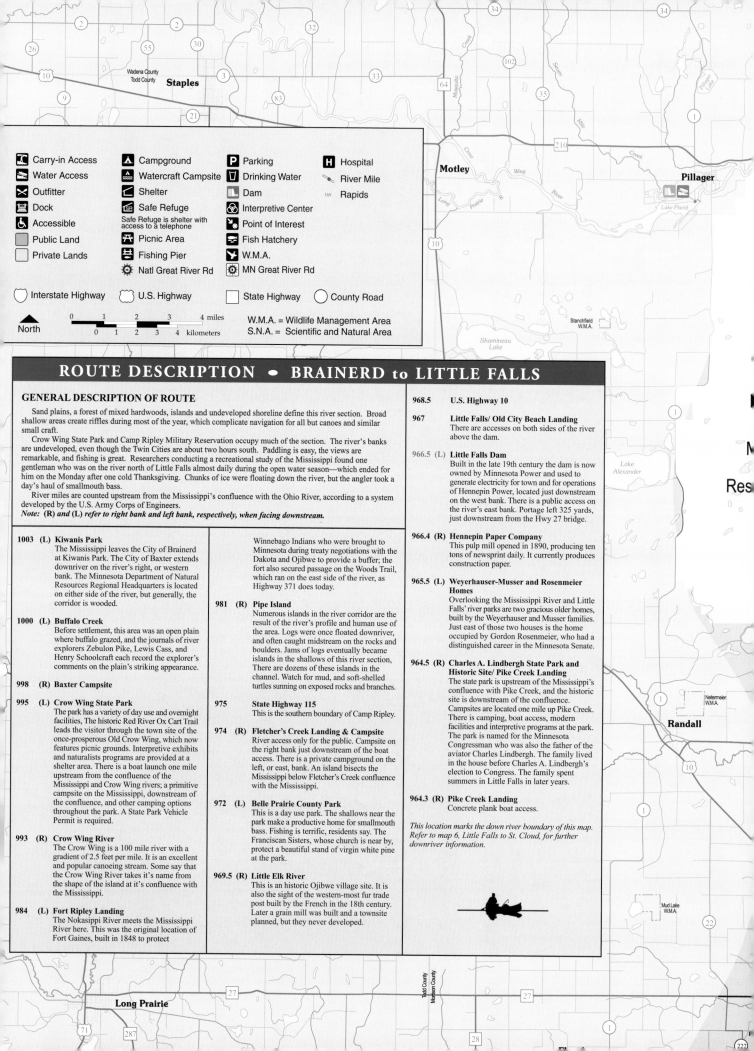

## Legend

- **Carry-in Access**
- **Water Access**
- **Outfitter**
- **Dock**
- **Accessible**
- **Public Land**
- **Private Lands**
- **Campground**
- **Watercraft Campsite**
- **Shelter**
- **Safe Refuge**
  Safe Refuge is shelter with access to a telephone
- **Picnic Area**
- **Fishing Pier**
- **Natl Great River Rd**
- **Parking**
- **Drinking Water**
- **Dam**
- **Interpretive Center**
- **Point of Interest**
- **Fish Hatchery**
- **W.M.A.**
- **MN Great River Rd**
- **Hospital**
- **River Mile**
- **Rapids**

**Interstate Highway**  **U.S. Highway**  **State Highway**  **County Road**

**North**

0 1 2 3 4 miles
0 1 2 3 4 kilometers

W.M.A. = Wildlife Management Area
S.N.A. = Scientific and Natural Area

# ROUTE DESCRIPTION • BRAINERD to LITTLE FALLS

## GENERAL DESCRIPTION OF ROUTE

Sand plains, a forest of mixed hardwoods, islands and undeveloped shoreline define this river section. Broad shallow areas create riffles during most of the year, which complicate navigation for all but canoes and similar small craft.

Crow Wing State Park and Camp Ripley Military Reservation occupy much of the section. The river's banks are undeveloped, even though the Twin Cities are about two hours south. Paddling is easy, the views are remarkable, and fishing is great. Researchers conducting a recreational study of the Mississippi found one gentleman who was on the river north of Little Falls almost daily during the open water season—which ended for him on the Monday after one cold Thanksgiving. Chunks of ice were floating down the river, but the angler took a day's haul of smallmouth bass.

River miles are counted upstream from the Mississippi's confluence with the Ohio River, according to a system developed by the U.S. Army Corps of Engineers.

*Note: (R) and (L) refer to right bank and left bank, respectively, when facing downstream.*

**1003 (L) Kiwanis Park**
The Mississippi leaves the City of Brainerd at Kiwanis Park. The City of Baxter extends downriver on the river's right, or western bank. The Minnesota Department of Natural Resources Regional Headquarters is located on either side of the river, but generally, the corridor is wooded.

**1000 (L) Buffalo Creek**
Before settlement, this area was an open plain where buffalo grazed, and the journals of river explorers Zebulon Pike, Lewis Cass, and Henry Schoolcraft each record the explorer's comments on the plain's striking appearance.

**998 (R) Baxter Campsite**

**995 (L) Crow Wing State Park**
The park has a variety of day use and overnight facilities, The historic Red River Ox Cart Trail leads the visitor through the town site of the once-prosperous Old Crow Wing, which now features picnic grounds. Interpretive exhibits and naturalists programs are provided at a shelter area. There is a boat launch one mile upstream from the confluence of the Mississippi and Crow Wing rivers; a primitive campsite on the Mississippi, downstream of the confluence, and other camping options throughout the park. A State Park Vehicle Permit is required.

**993 (R) Crow Wing River**
The Crow Wing is a 100 mile river with a gradient of 2.5 feet per mile. It is an excellent and popular canoeing stream. Some say that the Crow Wing River takes it's name from the shape of the island at it's confluence with the Mississippi.

**984 (L) Fort Ripley Landing**
The Nokasippi River meets the Mississippi River here. This was the original location of Fort Gaines, built in 1848 to protect

Winnebago Indians who were brought to Minnesota during treaty negotiations with the Dakota and Ojibwe to provide a buffer; the fort also secured passage on the Woods Trail, which ran on the east side of the river, as Highway 371 does today.

**981 (R) Pipe Island**
Numerous islands in the river corridor are the result of the river's profile and human use of the area. Logs were once floated downriver, and often caught midstream on the rocks and boulders. Jams of logs eventually became islands in the shallows of this river section, There are dozens of these islands in the channel. Watch for mud, and soft-shelled turtles sunning on exposed rocks and branches.

**975 State Highway 115**
This is the southern boundary of Camp Ripley.

**974 (R) Fletcher's Creek Landing & Campsite**
River access only for the public. Campsite on the right bank just downstream of the boat access. There is a private campground on the left, or east, bank. An island bisects the Mississippi below Fletcher's Creek confluence with the Mississippi.

**972 (L) Belle Prairie County Park**
This is a day use park. The shallows near the park make a productive home for smallmouth bass. Fishing is terrific, residents say. The Franciscan Sisters, whose church is near by, protect a beautiful stand of virgin white pine at the park.

**969.5 (R) Little Elk River**
This is an historic Ojibwe village site. It is also the sight of the western-most fur trade post built by the French in the 18th century. Later a grain mill was built and a townsite planned, but they never developed.

**968.5 U.S. Highway 10**

**967 Little Falls/ Old City Beach Landing**
There are accesses on both sides of the river above the dam.

**966.5 (L) Little Falls Dam**
Built in the late 19th century the dam is now owned by Minnesota Power and used to generate electricity for town and for operations of Hennepin Power, located just downstream on the west bank. There is a public access on the river's east bank. Portage left 325 yards, just downstream from the Hwy 27 bridge.

**966.4 (R) Hennepin Paper Company**
This pulp mill opened in 1890, producing ten tons of newsprint daily. It currently produces construction paper.

**965.5 (L) Weyerhauser-Musser and Rosenmeier Homes**
Overlooking the Mississippi River and Little Falls' river parks are two gracious older homes, built by the Weyerhauser and Musser families. Just east of those two houses is the home occupied by Gordon Rosenmeier, who had a distinguished career in the Minnesota Senate.

**964.5 (R) Charles A. Lindbergh State Park and Historic Site/ Pike Creek Landing**
The state park is upstream of the Mississippi's confluence with Pike Creek, and the historic site is downstream of the confluence. Campsites are located one mile up Pike Creek. There is camping, boat access, modern facilities and interpretive programs at the park. The park is named for the Minnesota Congressman who was also the father of the aviator Charles Lindbergh. The family lived in the house before Charles A. Lindbergh's election to Congress. The family spent summers in Little Falls in later years.

**964.3 (R) Pike Creek Landing**
Concrete plank boat access.

*This location marks the down river boundary of this map. Refer to map 6, Little Falls to St. Cloud, for further downriver information.*

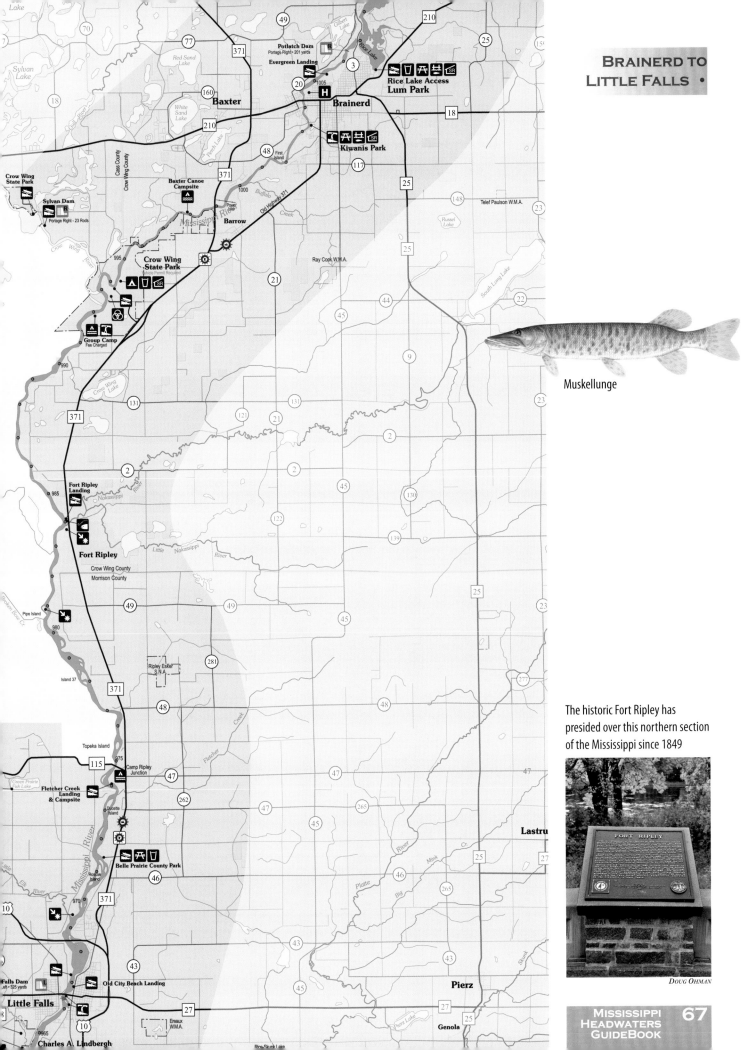

Muskellunge

The historic Fort Ripley has presided over this northern section of the Mississippi since 1849

*DOUG OHMAN*

Killdeer

The grassland prairie is a distinctive vegetative community of this river section. This prairie formed on dry sands located in outwash plains, old dune blankets, and alluvial deposits along the river. This soil is poor in nutrients and organic matter. Water drains quickly from it. Just as the open wetland or marsh builds up a mat of decaying vegetation that limits other plants, the meadow grasses of the prairie build a mat that slows the growth of trees and shrubs. The resulting plains of grass were once important grazing spots for large mammals, and were a neutral zone for Native Americans, so that all groups could hunt for their bands' needs.

The Mississippi's channel is underlain by sandbars and interrupted by islands that create riffles and make navigation difficult for even the smallest boat motor. These riffles create standing waves in the channel. The system of riffles begins at Pike Island, about three river miles below the Nokasippi, and continues downriver to the Morrison County Road 115 bridge, which is the southern boundary of Camp Ripley, a training facility owned and managed by the Minnesota National Guard. The rapids at Belle Prairie county park is a good place to observe the river channel.

Below the confluence with the Nokasippi River, the Mississippi River flows through a flat

"I started out thinking of America as highways and state lines. As I got to know it better, I began to think of it as rivers. Most of what I love about the country is a gift of the rivers. . . . America is a great story, and there is a river on every page of it."

—Charles Kuralt, On the Road

DOUG OHMAN

valley formed by glacial outwash material that is now bounded by hills on either side. The original prairies bordering the river were three to five miles long and one mile wide. These sandy plains were covered by prairie plants, and several species adapted to open and dry areas, like the prairie vole and upland sandpiper, which still live here.

A prominent glacial feature of this river section is the "Ripley esker," just east of the Mississippi and south of the Nokasippi River. This is a sinuous ridge created by the deposit of sediments by a stream running under a glacier. Water rushing under the melting glacier carved a channel that filled with sand, gravel, and rocks, leaving the ridge of debris when the glacier melted away. The Ripley esker stands up to 60 feet above the surrounding plain, is about 200 feet wide, and about six miles long.

It was formed by material deposited by glaciers moving into the region from the Lake Superior basin. Geologists found reddish volcanic and sedimentary rocks indicative of Lake Superior, as well as Lake Superior agate. The best views of the esker are in the spring and fall, when the trees have no leaves and the prairie grasses are in bloom. It is located near the intersection of Highway 371 and County Road 282.

As the name of the town (Little Falls) suggests, the Mississippi River fell over a series of rapids in this section, extending seven miles from the confluence with Pike Creek to the Two Rivers. Nicollet reports these were the Rapide Couteau, or Knife or Cutting Rapids, since the rocks cut up the canoes that tried to pass over them. From the rapids at the confluence of the Two Rivers, Nicollet's 1836 party traveled upriver, crossing other rapids, usually at the point where streams entered from the west. This relatively short journey took the group five hours, of which a quarter of the time was spent resting from the ascent of the previous rapids.

*DOUG OHMAN*

The Blanchard Dam in Little Falls

Blanchard Dam impounds the river and the rapids are flooded. But it is possible for the visitor to see some of the rocks that formed the rapids. The rock is a formation of mica schist, phyllite, and slate, rock which has metamorphosed from sedimentary materials, and is geologically similar to those visible at St. Anthony Falls, down river at Minneapolis. Another outcropping of this formation is visible at Charles A. Lindbergh State Park, located at the confluence with Pike Creek. The bed of the creek under the swing bridge on Lone Eagle Trail is covered with boulders that are fragments of this bedrock formation and other types of rocks imported by the glacier, including large granite erratics.

Nicollet was a French scientist and geologist, employed by the United States War Department to follow the Mississippi River and add to the measurements and surveys conducted by Schoolcraft and others. He was a fine observer of natural and human aspects of the landscape, and his journals of the trip paint word pictures that enable the

DOUG OHMAN

Historic Clemment Beaulieu house, moved back to its original spot at Old Crow Wing townsite in 1988. The townsite had been planned to be the main crossing of the railroad until the rail line realized it could build its bridge far less expensively by moving its placement a few miles north (now Brainerd).

reader to see the river and the people he met. One afternoon a group of Ojibwe women and children came to bid him farewell before they headed upriver to Leech Lake. Nicollet fretted with worry as they pulled away from the shore:

"I distribute several measures of ribbon, and the little flotilla composed of seven bark canoes recrosses the river. I watch with anxiety the orange line formed by these light gondolas checkered with hieroglyphics painted native style. I fear it might be cut off by the south wind that is blowing quite strongly. No, God protects these innocent navigators! The orange line becomes shorter and shorter. Each dot detaching itself vanishes into the reeds. There goes the last one. I sigh with relief."

At the base of a series of rapids near Little Falls, Nicollet's party spotted a unique mineral in the river bank:

"I noticed on the bank trickles of water oozing from under the rocks, suspending a kind of blue sand, brilliant, very fine, and sustaining afloat a matter very soft and oily to the touch when one stirred the liquid. It is a talcous sand resulting from the dissolution of a steatitic schist, rich in infinitely small talcum flakes, all filtering the oozing water referred to above.

This simple circumstance brings with it the opportunity of reflecting upon the relative value attached by the human species to objects supplied by nature for its needs. William, the trader, the merchant, saw in it a veritable gold mine, and among the natives it awakened the ideas of pleasure and vanity, inciting them to knead the sand, thus creating colors with which they daubed their faces, arms, and hair and smeared their foreheads, their clothing and their canoes."

The record of cultural use extends to the Paleoindian period. Nicollet, and the other Europeans who came upriver past this point noted a distinctive relic of this culture. At the upper end of the reach—near Mill Island in the present day river—"a rock eight to ten feet high is to be seen on the left (west) bank. Its vertical façade bears Indian inscriptions drawn with red chalk." Two of Nicollet's native guides then engaged in a lengthy discussion of the meaning of the inscription—"two bars more or less vertically parallel, followed by a circle under which was drawn a closed hand seizing something."

The younger of the two guides thought the rock's message was that a party of Ojibwe were descending the river, and in two days would shake hands with someone important, perhaps the Indian agent. The older of the two guides chided the other, and reminded him that the message was for the Dakota, and told them that the body of a band member had been recovered from the spot, where it had lain for three days and then was removed by the message writer and taken down river. "Finally, don't you remember they held dances for several days at Leech Lake when the head of hair was brought there?" he concluded.

The rock's position and its messages—without the benefit of translation—were recorded by Pike, Schoolcraft, Beltrami, and by Warren Upham in the state's geological survey.

## What communities do: Managing municipal and industrial wastes and providing drinking water

The Mississippi River was a natural location for a town. Prairies, woods, and the power of the river drew people to this section. "To enable you to manufacture your wares, nature made Little Falls," exhorted William H. Breyfogle in 1888. Breyfogle was the president of the Little Falls Power Company, which built the dam and power plant that launched the city's industrial development. Minnesota Power operated the power dam more recently. A sawmill and later a paper mill operated at the dam site. Hennepin Paper was a major employer for nearly 100 years, closing in the 1990s. The plant has been removed and today a park marks the point of Breyfogle's inspiration.

Regulating the discharge of sewage or wastes to rivers has been the focus of the nation's clean water laws. Management of rivers began as a commerce issue: limiting what is discharged to rivers was fully put into law with passage of the Clean Water Act in 1973.

Prior to then, the nation's rivers were literally sewers, collecting and transporting the wastes of the cities located on them. In the days before the law's provisions took effect, the river was a testament to the community's commerce. For example, someone fishing below the paper mills at Grand Rapids, Brainerd, or Little Falls usually hauled in

"Praise be, my Lord, for Sister Water... who is most useful, humble, precious, and chaste."
—St. Francis of Assisi, The Canticle of the Sun

DOUG OHMAN

paper waste on a fishing line. When buildings were constructed on the Mississippi for the Teacher's College at St. Cloud, the windows were turned away from the river because of the stench during the low water season.

In the 1960s and 1970s, the nation set water quality standards and sponsored an aggressive program to build wastewater treatment plants. These two acts resulted in huge reductions of waste and pollutants in the nation's rivers, from their passage in 1973 into the 21st century. Treating wastewater is a significant use for rivers, and it is especially critical for rivers that serve multiple purposes, such as the Mississippi—drinking water for one-quarter of Minnesota's residents, refuge for the nation's waterfowl, significant fishery and recreational and transportation hub for the Twin Cities. Is it possible to have it all, especially as population increases?

The University of Minnesota is working in partnership with the state Pollution Control Agency and businesses to develop new approaches to managing wastewater. Historically, industrial pretreatment programs have focused on end-of-pipe solutions to control the discharge of wastewater pollutants. Waste-

Little Falls

Only want sets a limit to waste.
—*Latin Proverb*

DOUG OHMAN

water treatment and pretreatment systems require both high capital and operating expenditures and do not eliminate or reduce wastes.

Today, cities and businesses are taking it to the next level by exploring ways to prevent pollution from entering the river. Pollution prevention incorporates practices that reduce the use of raw materials, water, and energy. Besides protecting the environment and conserving natural resources, companies have many financial incentives to implement pollution prevention programs, including cost savings related to raw materials, lost product, water, energy, and waste treatment and disposal. Implementing pollution prevention practices can also reduce a company's environmental liability and improve its public image.

Pollution prevention programs benefit wastewater operators by:

• Maximizing existing sewer and treatment capacity to avoid further investments in water supply and treatment infrastructure

• Reducing chemical, energy, and sludge management costs

• Improving biosolids quality through reduced loading of heavy metals

• Helping to meet the increasingly strict National Pollutant Discharge Elimination System (NPDES) permit limits by reducing wastewater loading from industrial users

• Strengthening local industry by helping businesses reduce wastes, cut costs, and meet regulatory requirements

• Minimizing risk of damage to pipes and sewage treatment equipment from industrial solvents and corrosives, thus reducing costs

• Lessening workplace exposure of toxic chemicals to Publicly Owned Treatment Works employees

• Protecting drinking water sources in the community by minimizing discharge of contaminants, especially in wellhead protection areas

*DOMINIQUE BRAUD*

Sandhill Cranes

## Lesson 5—Managing storm water—use rain barrels, install rain gardens, and work with natural design

The simplest way to manage rivers is to retain or mimic the river's functions in dissipating high water on a flood plain or absorbing nutrients and pollutants in riparian areas. Crow Wing and Morrison counties address this fundamental issue in their local water plans and comprehensive land use plans. These counties are at the forefront of addressing the pollution challenges of the 21st century—reducing the impact of storm water moving from developed areas into rivers.

"When a watershed is paved, it sheds water like a raincoat," states a Crow Wing County shoreland management fact sheet.

Just as wastewater discharged from point sources impaired water quality in the 1960s and 1970s, today the greatest source of pollution in rivers comes from overland runoff caused by storm water. This is known as nonpoint source pollution. Rainwater and snowmelt will always seek the lowest point in the landscape. Removing vegetation, changing land use from pasture to row crops, or hardening surfaces by laying down asphalt are all ways that accelerate the rate at which storm

"The children must be drawn towards and not away from the woods and fields and waters. They must be led to see more clearly that a man cut off from fellowship with the creatures of the open air is like a tree deprived of all its lateral roots and trimmed to a single branch. He may grow down and up, but he cannot grow out."

—*Stephen Forbes, Founder and first chief of the Natural History Survey*

Highway 371 bridge, entry to Baxter

water enters a river. These changes also eliminate the natural functions of absorbing storm water through soils, depressions, or rooted vegetation.

The shoreland manager's job is to first understand what the likely storm water amount is for a given location during a typical year, and then to assure that the development either stops or absorbs that amount of runoff and does not allow it to flow directly into streams and rivers.

A rain barrel is the simplest way for an individual property owner to reduce the flow of rainwater.

A rain garden intercepts the flow of storm water and absorbs some and treats some.

A vegetated buffer on a stream bank or lake shoreline also reduces overland flow and absorbs nutrients.

The Lakes Area Clean Water Council calls these practices: "drop, stop, and absorb." They are relatively simple for the individual property owner to install. Property owners building on lots smaller than allowed by current zoning are often required to adopt these practices.

www.dropstopabsorb.org/index.html

The same principles apply to commercial and business building and development, although the scale must be consistent with the square footage of the building.

*Doug Ohman*

As a provider of industry, jobs, tourism, recreation, drinking water, and inspiration to our societies for thousands of years, the Mississippi River deserves our continued respect and consideration.

*Doug Ohman*

*Doug Ohman*

HERE 1475 FT
ABOVE
THE OCEAN
THE MIGHTY
MISSISSIPPI
BEGINS
TO FLOW
ON ITS
WINDING WAY
2552 MILES
TO THE
GULF OF
MEXICO

"The River itself has no beginning or end.  In its beginning, it is not yet the River; in its end, it is no longer the River.  What we call the headwaters is only a selection from among the innumerable sources which flow together to compose it.  At what point in its course does the Mississippi become what the Mississippi means?"

—*T. S. Eliot*

As we have traveled down the river figuretively in this book, it is the authors' and publishers' hope that we can all, in reality, spend more time on the banks and/or the waters of this river. For it is in this time spent with the river that we come to understand and appreciate it's true wealth and value to our predecessors, ourselves, but even more importantly–the generations to come.

Following are some suggestions to encourage more exploration of the headwaters of the Mississippi River.

## Review Section - Five things to know about and see in the headwaters

All along the headwaters of the Mississippi, the towns and cities offer comfortable camping, supplies, shopping, and historical sites to the traveler, whether traveling by roads or the river itself.

### Lake Itasca to Cass Lake

This river section is the Mississippi's source. It includes the most remote and hard to reach sections of the river and the first city on the Mississippi—Bemidji. The visitor will learn about the glacial origins of the state's topography. It is also a place to learn about all the people who have lived on the river since the glaciers melted.

Schoolcraft Island on Lake Itasca is a special place in this river section. It is an easy paddle or boat ride from the recreational service vendors located on the lake's northeast shore, within Itasca State Park. Henry Schoolcraft camped here in July 1832, on his voyage to discover the Mississippi's headwaters. He and his companions made a flagstaff and left a small flag, which they could observe as they paddled north from the island and down the Mississippi from its source.

This section is also where one can begin to understand the reservoir system designed with channels, dams, and lakes (Cass, Leech, Winnebigoshish, etc.) to manage a relatively controlled amount of water being sent down the river, determined by spring melts, rains, or droughts.

### Cass Lake to Schoolcraft

This river section is the Mississippi's northern reach. The visitor will experience broad savannahs of wetlands laid down on glacial outwash, contrasted with towering forests of red and white pine. This section is homeland to the Leech Lake Band of Ojibwe who have lived on and near the Mississippi since long before Minnesota was a state.

On Cass Lake, Star Island is said to be one of the only islands within the continental United States that includes its own lake–Windigo Lake.

This river section is home also to the nation's largest population of breeding bald eagles, protected in part because of the work of biologists of the Chippewa National Forest. Cut Foot Sioux Interpretive Center, on the northeast shore of Lake Winnibigoshish, is a relic from the Woodland period of human occupation, managed by the U.S. Forest Service. An excellent side trip is to Cut Foot Sioux Lake on the northeastern side of Lake Winnibigoshish, the location of the Turtle and Snake Indian Mounds. One mound is in the shape of a turtle, about 25 by 30 feet, with the head pointing north; around the mound is a snake with the head and tail meeting and pointing south.

The turtle signifies the Dakota's victory over the Ojibwe, who moved into the area during the fur trade. The turtle's head points north, the direction that the Dakota drove their enemy. The snake, built a year later, shows the Ojibwe returned and defeated their enemy. Its head points south, the direction that the Dakota took, and where the Ojibwe continued to expand.

*DOMINIQUE BRAUD*

Common Merganzer

Frog Tadpole

"Night and day the river flows. If time is the mind of space, the River is the soul of the desert. Brave boatmen come, they go, they die, the voyage flows on forever. We are all canyoneers. We are all passengers on this little mossy ship, this delicate dory sailing round the sun that humans call the earth. **Joy**, shipmates, **joy**."

—*Edward Abbey, The Hidden Canyon -- A River Journey*

If you paddle downstream from Winnibigoshish, you will see the white sands on the river bottom and its shorelines that blew into the area during a hot and dry period thousands of years ago.

### Schoolcraft State Park to Palisade

This river section starts in forests and wetlands, rushes over bedrock, and ends in a long meandering course across the ancient lake plain of Glacial Lake Aitkin. The rocks that made Grand Rapids are flooded by the Pokegama Dam. You can see outcroppings of the bedrock that underlies the northeastern corner of the state if you visit Portage Park, near Cohasset and upstream of Grand Rapids. This is the southern tip of the "Canadian Shield."

### Palisade to Brainerd

This river section skirts the southwesterly extension of Minnesota's iron range. A series of hills southeast of the river are drumlins—debris dumped by glaciers lying on a similar axis. French Rapids is a dramatic compression of the river, just upstream of Brainerd. This portion of the river is relatively easy to navigate as it widens due to its many tributaries.

### Brainerd to Little Falls

In Morrison County, below the Mississippi's confluence with the Crow Wing River, the Mississippi connects the state's three biological regions—the prairies to the west, the conifers to the north, and the hardwoods of the east. The aptly named Belle Prairie was long a place where people gathered. The Mississippi River here boasts the best water quality and the best location for aquatic life. The Belle Prairie County Park is a place to see both rapids and history.

Just 7 miles north of Little Falls, north of County 48 on the east side of Highway 371, lies a wonderful example of a deposit left behind by the same glaciers that carved the lakes and rivers of our region. A geological marker is found on the site next to the entrance of the Ripley Esker. To best view this formation, visit in early spring or late fall when the trees have no leaves and the prairie grasses have cured.

*CHIP BORKENHAGEN*

The Ripley Esker

### Resources - For more information:

The Ripley Esker
www.dnr.state.mn.us/snas/sna00959/index.html
Minnesota Department of Natural Resources
About Watersheds
www.dnr.state.mn.us/watersheds/index.html
Healthy Rivers: A Water Course
www.dnr.state.mn.us/healthyrivers/index.html
Minnesota Pollution Control Agency
www.pca.state.mn.us/index.php/water/water-types-and-programs/surface-water/basins-and-watersheds/basins-and-watersheds-in-minnesota.html
U.S. Environmental Protection Agency
www.water.epa.gov/type/watersheds/index.cfm

*The Mississippi carries an average of 436,000 tons of sediment each day. Over the course of a year, it moves an average of 159 million tons of sediment.*

"Water is the most critical resource issue of our lifetime and our children's lifetime. The health of our waters is the principal measure of how we live on the land."
—Luna Leopold

"Water flows over these hands.
May I use them skillfully
to preserve our precious planet."
—Thich Nhat Hanh,
Earth Prayers from Around the World

Itasca

Pine Martin

Woodland Sunflower